A POLITICS

OF THE

COMMON GOOD

A POLITICS
OF THE
COMMON GOOD

PATRICK RIORDAN SJ

INSTITUTE OF PUBLIC ADMINISTRATION

First published 1996
by the Institute of Public Administration,
57–61 Lansdowne Road,
Dublin, Ireland.

British Library Cataloguing in Publication Data

ISBN 1 872002 43 9

Cover design by Butler Claffey Design, Dun Laoghaire

Typeset by Wendy Commins, The Curragh
Printed by Leinster Leader, Naas, Co. Kildare.

CONTENTS

	Acknowledgements	vi
	Introduction	1
1	The Common Good: Locating the Problem	6
2	An Alternative Rationality	28
3	Is Altruism the Key to the Common Good?	44
4	The Common Good of Practices	50
5	Another Look at Public Order	76
6	Rights and Public Order	104
7	The Debate on the Human Good	116
8	Securing a Public Space	127
9	Discourse and the Process of Politics	136
10	The Language of the Common Good	153
	Notes	171
	Index	181

ACKNOWLEDGEMENTS

The argument of this book has been worked out over a number of years through the discussion of current political issues. Some of the material included in its chapters has been published in other form in journals or elsewhere. I am grateful to editors for permission to reproduce, and acknowledge my debt to them. Material in Chapters 3, 5 and 6 appeared in *Studies*; material included in Chapters 2 and 9 appeared in *Milltown Studies*; Chapter 10 is a reworking of an article which appeared in *Landas*, Journal of Loyola School of Theology, Manila; and Chapter 5 also includes some material previously published in *Administration* and *The Irish Philosophical Journal.* Material on models of punishment in Chapter 1 is taken from a paper delivered to a conference on punishment under the auspices of the Council for Social Welfare which intends to publish the papers. The discussion of the public space for debate was first presented in a contribution to *Divorce? Facing the Issues of Marital Breakdown* edited by Mags O'Brien (Dublin: Basement Press, 1995).

I am very grateful to my brother, Liam, to Fr Tom McGrath, SJ, and to Frank Litton and Tony McNamara of the Institute of Public Administration whose helpful comments on earlier drafts enabled me to become clearer in my own mind at least what it is I want to say. No doubt I shall discover from readers' comments the extent to which my argument is still in need of clarification. And finally a particular word of thanks to my friends, without whom I would have no inkling of our common goods.

INTRODUCTION

D oes Ireland need a new constitution? Is it time to replace the 1937 constitution in order to respond to political developments in relation to Northern Ireland and social and cultural developments in the country as a whole? The recent series of referenda to amend the constitution in order to address matters of social legislation provokes this reflection. The government has responded by establishing a commission to investigate the need for a review of the constitution. However, the debate has already begun, and opinions on what should be deleted from the old and what should be incorporated in the new can already be heard.

One opinion which is frequently expressed is that any part of the language of the 1937 constitution which is distinctively Catholic needs to be replaced by a more general language that is capable of being accepted by all citizens, whatever their religious allegiance. The concern behind this opinion is well articulated by the American political philosopher, John Rawls, in his recent book *Political Liberalism*.[1] In a pluralist society, in which citizens are divided by reasonable though incompatible religious, philosophical and moral doctrines, what basis can there be for their cooperation in maintaining a system of law and of government? The comprehensive philosophical or religious world-view of any one group as a basis for political and legal order could not expect to evoke allegiance from adherents of other comprehensive doctrines. It would seem that an overlapping consensus in support of the basic structures of a political and legal system could only be achieved by an articulation of that order which was not tied to any one comprehensive doctrine yet was capable of receiving the support of all.

This is the question which is surfacing in Ireland today in regard to its constitution. Is the language of the 1937 constitution the property of one religious world-view and therefore incapable of expressing the overlapping consensus of a pluralist society? In this book, I examine the notion of the common good, a term which occurs frequently in the constitution. How does it rate when examined in this light? Does one have to be a Catholic in order to understand the concept and use it? It is probably accurate to say that the concept is most used today in Catholic Church documents, such as the 1995 papal encyclical on the value of human life, *Evangelium Vitae.*[2] But while such a remark might be appropriate to the sociology of knowledge it would be logically mistaken to take it as justifying the conclusion that the notion of the common good is only intelligible and useful to Catholics. The question must remain open.

The question is often asked polemically: is the concept of the common good a sectarian concept? This formulation of the question seems to imply that concepts which are at home in a Catholic world-view are sectarian. Some will be offended by this suggestion. It is important to understand before taking offence. The word 'sectarian' is used nowadays in contexts very different from the original theological origins of the term. Within theology a sect is taken to refer to a small group which diverges from the doctrinal mainstream of a major church. Sects are regarded as deviant forms of the religious group, and are often characterised by biblical fundamentalism, a rigorous ethical system and anti-institutional tendencies.[3] Theologically speaking, sects are groups which diverge from mainstream churches. But in contemporary journalistic and even philosophical usage the word sectarian is used to label expressions of any religious content in relation to the political sphere.

It is not difficult to understand what is at stake here. Within pluralist societies that are made up of groups of differing and even conflicting religious and philosophical views, there is no possibility of achieving commitment by each citizen to a civil and political system if that system is identified with only one of the competing groups. There is need for a language to express the rationale of the civil and political order which is accessible to all citizens equally. Much of the literature in the contemporary political philosophical debate is devoted to finding and clarifying the necessary language. A recent book by an Irish political philosopher, Attracta Ingram of University College Dublin, states the problem well: we have a 'political interest in finding a shared starting point for constructing political arrangements for citizens who have diverse moral traditions and substantive ideals of human flourishing'.[4] Is there a way of articulating the rationale of civil society and of the state in such a way that they can receive the allegiance of reasonable citizens who do not agree with one another on fundamental issues of a religious and philosophical nature? Ingram remarks further that all citizens must recognise that 'from the point of view of others their own perspective is but one more sectarian doctrine of final ends'.[5] Here we have a use of the term sectarian in a purely political context. It refers to principles and values which are incapable of achieving consensus in a pluralist society, because they belong to one of a number of contending positions.

It is in this sense that the question about the common good is asked. Does this concept disqualify itself from the political forum because of its ancestry? In this book I argue that the concept of the common good is not sectarian in the qualified sense, that it is capable of being understood and used by citizens who otherwise hold differing values and convictions, and that it is in fact a necessary concept if we are to handle problems which arise when the models we use for explaining cooperation are too restrictive. Ingram's book is devoted to expounding a political theory of rights, that is, a theory of rights which is capable of evoking consensus in a pluralist society. The need for a doctrine of rights arises 'because, as citizens of modern republics, we meet as strangers without a common good except whatever we can forge together for the

advancement of our diverse ends'.[6] The possibility of constructing a doctrine of rights, and of establishing that doctrine on a
shared understanding of the autonomy of the citizen, suggests
that there is the possibility of a common good precisely in the
context of the overlapping consensus of reasonable citizens
in a pluralist society. In this book I will attempt to explain the
concept of the common good and show how it is relevant and
useful for reflection on a liberal democracy in a pluralist
society.

My argument can be briefly stated: we have to pay attention
to the way in which we think about our social interaction.
We have been taught to think about it in terms of the pursuit
of self-interest. But this way of thinking leads us to act in ways
which undermine social cohesion. Our experience of social
life reveals possibilities of cooperating in the pursuit of common goals, and so there is a need for a language and for an
explanatory model which is adequate to this experience.
Chapter 1 discusses punishment in order to illustrate how the
way in which we think impacts on what we do. I contrast different ways of thinking, one way which assumes conflict
between individuals whose interests are incompatible with one
another, and another which assumes a certain communality
of interest and activity. I hope to show that the assumption of
conflict between isolated individuals would in fact contribute
to us both interpreting and constructing social interaction in
terms of conflict. The expectation of conflict would be a self-
fulfilling prophecy, leading to a fostering of conflict and a corresponding diminishment in social cohesion.

In Chapter 2 I examine the model of thinking based on
the assumption of self-interest. The limitations exposed in this
model point us in the direction of the need for analyses which
allow for shared or common interests. Chapter 3 excludes the
notion of altruism as the appropriate alternative to self-interest,
and Chapter 4 explores the possibility of understanding cooperation in terms of practices. This leads to an understanding
of social institutions as common goods, because of the way in
which they enable people and groups to achieve the internal
goods that they seek in practices. I develop this thought to

elaborate the notion of public order as the common good of politics. While public order would have to include more than the minimal shared interests presupposed by traditionally liberal analyses, it would not include a comprehensive treatment of the human good. The particular institutions of the liberal state are discussed in Chapter 5 in relation to the notion of public order. Chapter 6 continues this line of investigation in considering human rights. Issues arising from the consideration of public order and of the content of rights suggest that the common good of liberal politics includes a consideration of elements of the human good. This is the topic of Chapter 7. In Chapter 8 I argue that the common good of political community would include the maintenance of a space for debate on aspects of the human good. Chapter 9 considers the conditions to ensure a certain quality of participation in that debate, so that it would not deteriorate finally into mere bargaining. The conditions to be maintained would have to include the capacities of citizens for participation in discourse free from domination, and the forms of education and training to develop those capacities. In Chapter 10 it remains to spell out the language of the common good in order to see its strengths and weaknesses as an element of the overlapping consensus.

CHAPTER 1

THE COMMON GOOD: LOCATING THE PROBLEM

The argument of this book is twofold. It is both a critique of what is, and a search for what might be better. The critique examines the limitations of the language available to us for speaking of our cooperation in society. The suggested improvement explores the need for a rhetoric of the common good in relation to social cooperation. The language we use in speaking of social reality is multilayered and complex. It includes the common-sense terms and standards with which we will spontaneously answer questions like 'what are you doing? why are you doing that?'; but it also includes the more refined terminology and criteria developed by the human and social sciences for explaining human action and interaction. Of course, the two levels of common sense and science are not completely distinct. A common-sense account can provide part of the data for the anthropologists or sociologists, which their theories must explain. On the other hand, the theories developed by economists and sociologists can influence people's common-sense self-understanding by providing concepts and criteria that are adopted into everyday language. Terminology that had its origin in Freud's development of psychoanalysis or in Marx's analysis of the class structure of bourgeois society is now part of the language available for public debate.

This influence of the human sciences on ordinary language underpins the practical relevance of my investigation. My focus is not exclusively on one or other dimension of the language. Of course, the articulated models for explaining social cooperation used by the human sciences are more accessible; they involve terms and criteria which are explicitly formulated. But the investigation and critique applies also to the use of those models at the common-sense level. Accordingly, when I propose that the language of the common good is useful for speaking of cooperation, I am not merely considering the importance of increasing the explanatory power of the human sciences; I am also considering the enrichment of people's understanding of their everyday practice. And correspondingly, when I point out the restrictions implicit in the categories of analysis, I am also concerned with the impoverishment of self-understanding which results from the limitations of the language available for public debate.

The connection between the technical language generated for analysis and the self-understanding and behaviour of ordinary people was remarked upon by Jean Jacques Rousseau, the French eighteenth-century philosopher. In his famous discourse on the origins of social inequality he reflected on the impact which education in social thought had on the behaviour of people. He commented on how the process of socialisation including education in philosophy resulted in a loss of a sense of compassion with suffering fellow human beings. The consequences were that people in society no longer identified with the difficulties of others, but considered only their own interests. It is worth quoting him at length:

> Reason is what engenders egocentrism (*amour propre*), and reflection strengthens it. Reason is what turns man in upon himself. Reason is what separates him from all that troubles him and afflicts him. Philosophy is what isolates him and what moves him to say in secret, at the sight of a suffering man, 'Perish if you will; I am safe and sound.' No longer can anything but danger to the entire society trouble the tranquil slumber of the philosopher and yank him from his bed. His fellow man can be killed with impunity underneath his window. He has merely to place his hands over his ears and argue with himself a little in order to prevent nature, which rebels within him, from identifying him with the man being assassinated. Savage man does not have this admirable

talent, and for lack of wisdom and reason he is always seen
thoughtlessly giving in to the first sentiment of humanity. When
there is a riot or a street brawl, the populace gathers together;
the prudent man withdraws from the scene. It is the rabble, the
women of the marketplace, who separate the combatants and
prevent decent people from killing one another.[1]

Rousseau contrasts two kinds of response to the situation
of human need. One response is to come to the aid of those
suffering or in danger; the other is to avoid the disturbance
and ignore the appeals for help. Rousseau considers that the
helping response arises from a feeling of compassion or pity
which is natural to humans when they are not too sophisticated.
The other response becomes possible once the process of
socialisation has deadened the natural sentiment of identification with one's fellows in need. In that process of socialisation, as Rousseau sees it, reason, reflection and philosophy
play a significant role. Instead of philosophy and science
lending support to the socially valuable activity of aiding those
in need, they actually function so as to undermine people's
willingness in this regard. While Rousseau's analysis leads him
in a different direction, his comments on this scenario provide me with an illustration of the point I wish to make in this
book. I want to argue that the language and analysis provided
by much of the human sciences not only do not explain all of
our experience of cooperation, but actually contribute to
undermining our willingness to cooperate by fostering self-
understandings at the common-sense level which are inimical
to cooperation. What I wish to propose, therefore, is that
analysis of human social action in terms of the common good
not only would help us make sense of our experience of cooperation, but also would be more conducive to fostering
willing cooperation.

Rousseau relies on the feeling of pity or compassion in order
to make sense of the assistance given by some to others in
need. I am presuming that such socially useful activity is not
irrational, and that it can be explained in terms which do not
reduce to a mere expression of personal preference: 'I help
because I like helping'. It would be part of the task in the

elaboration of the common good to outline the rationality of such behaviour. Rousseau wants to expose the anti-social and alienating effect of reason and philosophy and so he mentions here only their negative potential. They are alienating in that they instil the habit of reflection in terms of one's own interests. Trained to consult self-interest, and to consider action rational only to the extent that it furthers one's interests, people are no longer able to see any point in what they formerly spontaneously did. A narrow understanding of rationality in terms of self-interest results in a labelling of perfectly good, socially useful, spontaneous cooperation as irrational. This restriction of rationality must be exposed and a broader conception elaborated.

Just as in Rousseau's time, the prevalent models of rationality in the human sciences today are predicated on self-interest. These models may not be intended as prescriptive models, recommending or commanding a certain form of action, but they inevitably become prescriptive, the more they influence the way in which participants interpret social experience. Bill Jordan, in a book entitled *The Common Good*, makes this point specifically about economic theories.[2] Built on minimal and generalised assumptions, the theories may be intended as descriptive, but when they gain acceptance, they provide the terms and criteria with which social actors interpret and construct the world. The more the social and economic world is constructed in their terms, the more necessary it becomes for people to conform to the criteria of rationality operative in the theory in order to be able to cope and succeed in that world. What starts out for the purposes of explanation as an abstracted, idealised model, functions indirectly as a normative guideline for people who wish to participate in the system, and then proves to be a predictor of behaviour. If there is empirical confirmation of the theory, then perhaps it is only because people have had to adjust their behaviour to the assumptions of the theory in order to cope in a world which is increasingly shaped by experts and technocrats. What purports to be purely descriptive functions prescriptively.

Coming to the aid of one in need is a particular instance of human cooperation suggested by Rousseau's remarks. As an example of cooperation in general, therefore, it is limited. Contemporary societies are built upon a wide range of far more complex forms of cooperation. How do participants in such cooperation make sense of their own action? And what resources are available to the scientific observer to explain and evaluate such cooperation? In what follows, I will rely on a discussion of the penal system to explore further the questions raised above: how do social actors understand their activity? How does the understanding of the scientific observer relate to that of the engaged participant? What significance has the notion of the common good in the understandings of participant and observer?

THE PENAL SYSTEM

A basic question of this book is 'how do citizens make sense of their participation in social cooperation?' A subsidiary but related question is 'how do public administrators make sense to themselves of their participation in structures of government?' Andrew Rutherford in his book *Criminal Justice and the Pursuit of Decency* attempts to answer this question in relation to professionals involved in the British penal system.[3] Rutherford worked as a prison officer in the UK prison service for ten years, and in the early seventies he shifted into academic work in the area of penology. He is author of several books in this field. This particular book is an investigation into the operative ideologies of practitioners in the prison service. Based on interviews with twenty-eight people in the police, probation and prison services, he formulated three typical 'working credos' which articulate the practitioners' view of the purpose of their work. The three are labelled the punishment, efficiency and caring credos.

(1)   The punishment credo is a cluster of ideas and values which include 'a powerfully held dislike and moral condemnation of offenders, and the beliefs that as few fetters as possible [should] be placed upon the authorities

in the pursuit of criminals who, when caught, should be dealt with in ways that are punitive and degrading'.[4] Rutherford quotes the nineteenth-century English judge, James Fitzjames Stephen, as typifying this attitude: 'I think it highly desirable that criminals should be hated, that the punishment inflicted on them should be so contrived as to give expression to that hatred'.[5]

(2) The efficiency credo is described as concentration upon the issues of management, pragmatism, efficiency and expedience. Rutherford quotes from an account of the inauguration of a new regime in an American prison to exemplify this credo: the new governor 'brought to the prison a commitment to scientific management rather than to any correctional ideology'; the governor 'is neither in favour of nor opposed to rehabilitation programs. His primary commitment is to running a safe, clean program-orientated institution which functions smoothly on a day-to-day basis and that is not in violation of code provisions, administrative regulations or court orders'.[6]

(3) The caring credo is an attitude towards suspects, accused persons and prisoners based on liberal and humanitarian values. It includes an optimism that constructive work can be done with offenders, a commitment to the rule of law so as to restrict state powers, and an insistence on open and accountable procedures.

The working credos are instanced in the texts of the interviews with prison governors, probation officers and police, and the ramifications and practical implications of these viewpoints are spelled out. There is a tendency among practitioners to adopt either the punishment or the efficiency credo due to their experience of disillusionment with the rehabilitation ideal which had predominated in the sixties and seventies. It was great confidence in the knowledge and competence of the graduates in the new social sciences which had led to the adoption of the rehabilitative ideal in penal policy, both in the US and in the UK. 'By about 1960, there was a strong liberal consensus of informed penal thought in

Britain, which believed that rapid strides would soon be made scientifically towards the identification of specific types of effective treatment for specific types of offender.'[7] The enthusiasm for the treatment of offenders with a view to their rehabilitation dissolved within a space of fifteen years according to Rutherford. He mentions three circumstances which largely account for the loss of faith in the rehabilitative ideal: studies done of the effectiveness of rehabilitation programmes drew negative conclusions; there was concern that sentencing and parole decisions guided by the rehabilitative ideal led to unfair treatment of some; and the practitioners of rehabilitation lost the moral high ground by their reliance on a language which seemed to make offenders things to be manipulated rather than people. Take for instance the following statement by one of his interviewees, a chief probation officer:

> I was an interventionist, to be honest, in a way that I am slightly appalled at now, because we did a lot of things then for extremely good motives that did not have a very good ending . . . With hindsight, I regret that we were so ready to intervene in people's lives. That phase was one of enormous confidence and a belief in a value of some of the positive things we were doing, but without the caution that comes with age and experience and about who you do it to.[8]

Rutherford does not simply write as an observer, offering an analysis of what goes on; rather he writes from the perspective of a participant, with commitment to a view of what should be going on. His preferred working credo is the third, and he would want this to be the operative ideology throughout the penal system. He warns that allowing the punitive and efficient credos to dominate in practice will lead to apathy among practitioners and ultimately violence in the system. The persuasion he is attempting is couched in the language of humane values which he hopes his colleagues will share, but he can rely on the self-understanding of those interviewees who described their work in the terms of the caring credo as evidence that his hope is not misplaced.[9] His book therefore is evidence that there are at least some possibilities of self-understanding other than those offered in terms of self-interest, contract, efficiency and control. There are some professionals in the criminal justice system who operate out of such an understanding and who want to persuade their colleagues to cooperate with them on those terms. It remains to be shown that the language of the common good can facilitate them in expressing their perspective.

MODELS OF PUNISHMENT

What difference would it make to an understanding of punishment to view it in terms of the common good? In what follows I hope to illustrate the usefulness of a language of the common good in making sense of punishment. Punishment is a part of human social experience. We all have had the experience of being punished, and many of us will have experience of punishing others. But like many other elements of human experience, it is difficult to speak about it. When we attempt to express the rationale of punishment, to explain what it is, and offer justification for punishments imposed, we frequently find ourselves at the limits of our language. We may have a basic intuitive sense that punishment is sometimes necessary, and that it can be a humanly good thing, but we may not have the concepts to express this sense and explain it. When an issue arises like the role of victims of crime in relation to punishment, we find that we need a coherent grasp of the point of punishment in order to be able to say where the victim fits in. But where are we to find an adequate theory of punishment? The literature provides us with a range of possible theories, which are usually distinguished from one another and presented in some detail.[10] The labels of deterrence, rehabilitation, retribution and incapacitation are familiar. Each theory seems plausible in its own terms. That is because each of those theories is derived from something very familiar to us. Each tends to focus on one area of our experience, and indeed on one aspect within that restricted area, and to use that situation to generate our basic concepts and principles. The situation we focus on becomes a model which we then rely on to deal with questions arising in other situations. I want to explore some of our models in relation to punishment, in order to illustrate the relevance of the language of the common good in this area.

What is meant by model? An architectural image may help. When the planners propose the development of some area they construct a model of the project, which images the proposed buildings and allows an overview of the whole in the context of its environment; the different parts can then be seen in relation to the whole and to one another. I am suggesting that our spontaneous thinking also operates with models, conceptual rather than physical, and that these models allow us to imagine and speak of totalities which we could not normally experience. The problem with our models is that while they claim to be applicable to the whole of a relevant area of experience, they are generated on the basis of some limited and restricted experience.

To return to the topic of punishment: in the broadest sense of a description we can say that punishment is a response to wrongdoing (or crime, or lawbreaking). Punishment in this sense occurs in child rearing, in sport, in the state, in the army, in various organisations and societies and in churches. There is a great variety of experience of punishment, and while we can identify some common elements, like 'response to wrong-doing', we should not underestimate the great differences between the different cases. The particular experiences of punishment are many and varied and they give rise to a variety of models. The models generated on the basis of these particular experiences may then appear to be applicable beyond their generating context across a wide spectrum of practical life. This extrapolation may be such as to conceal some aspect of reality or to impose inappropriate concepts on experience. I want to look at some of these various contexts of punishment and at the models they generate. I will consider models based on the correction of children and the restoration of fairness in a game, and models from the margins of social existence. I do not claim that this selection of models is exhaustive;

however, I discuss these because I find them clearly operative in current discussion and because they exhibit a radical difference of approach which also emerges in the context of the discussion of the role of victims in the punishment of offenders.

CORRECTION

Probably our earliest experience of punishment is of correction. As small children we were corrected when we misbehaved. Punishment as correction had a pedagogical point: it was to help us learn important lessons about how to orient ourselves in our physical and social environments. If we look at the kinds of behaviour by children which usually count as wrongdoing and therefore deserving punishment, we note that the behaviour frequently has no victim. Of course there are cases with victims, as when Mary monopolises the toys she is supposed to share with Jane. But Mary also is warned not to put her hand near the oven, not to cycle her tricycle off the footpath, not to get her good clothes dirty. Misbehaving in these cases has no victim; it may not even result in any harm to Mary, but yet she will be corrected. The point of the correction is that she should learn to conform to rules which are designed to protect her from harm. Some of these rules may refer to her social well-being and corresponding 'harm', as for instance the rules of etiquette. Mary will be corrected for bad table manners, behaviour which involves and affects her relationships with others, but which could hardly be said to have a victim. Examples could be multiplied. My point is simply to illustrate how this situation of common experience might provide an engendering model for a theory of punishment. It would lead us to see all punishment as essentially corrective, pedagogical in its point, focusing on the wrongdoer as one needing to learn, 'to be taught a lesson'! But of course with this engendering model, there is no consideration of victims, since the wrongful behaviour did not necessarily have a victim. Others might indeed come under consideration since the behaviour which is to be fostered by the correction is also oriented towards others, but the victims of previous misdeeds are not relevant.

Different circumstances and different cultures will require different and often mutually contradictory rules, because what is conducive to the physical and social well-being of individuals is to some extent at least relative to circumstances and culture. But those engaged in correction must share some view of the human good which it is the point of the rules and of punishment to foster. That good is a common good: recognised and shared by the administrators of correction and aimed at for those corrected. It is in order that they might attain this human good that children are corrected.

RESTORATION

Another common experience of punishment which might provide us with an engendering model is that within sport. Take a foul in the game of soccer as an example of wrongdoing and an awarded penalty as the punishment in response. What constitutes a foul is defined by the rules of the game; the wrongdoing in this case is also an infringement of rules. A defender who brings down an attacking opponent by a tackle off the ball commits a foul; if that foul takes place within a specified area in front of the goal-mouth (the penalty area), the attacking team will be awarded a penalty, that is, a direct kick at the goal-mouth defended only by the goalkeeper. In the normal case, a penalty very probably leads to a goal. In this example, the wrongdoing has victims. First of all the attacking forward who is brought down is a victim. He suffers the harm resulting from his fall, but also the deprivation of the opportunity to score, with his chances of excelling as a footballer, attaining recognition from his peers, and glory and adulation from his fans. But secondly, the attacking team as a whole is a victim of the foul. The team is united in cooperating with a view to scoring goals: that is where its interests lie, and those interests are negatively affected by the foul. The response to the foul by the referee, the adjudicating official, is to award a penalty to the attacking team. The penalty takes away from the defending team whatever advantage in the defence of its own goal-mouth it might have hoped to gain from the unlawful tackle. The temporary respite in defence is just that, temporary, and the attack is given renewed force. The penalty kick therefore restores to the attacking team the advantage which was taken from it in the foul.

This form of punishment is essentially restorative. It restores a pre-existing balance of fairness between the two teams which had been competing within the rules on the basis of skill and stamina until the foul had upset that balance. The balance of fairness constitutes equality in one very fundamental sense: the teams can be very unequal in terms of skill, experience, reputation, height and strength, but they are equal in relation to the rules and conditions which apply to their contest. That equality was undermined by the offender's attempt to gain an advantage for his team in a forbidden action. The punishment attempts a redistribution of advantage with a view to restoring the balance of fairness.[11]

We must be careful not to exaggerate the extent of the restoration. The history cannot be undone: what might have been without the interference of the foul remains just that, what might have been. The attacking forward who had been brought down receives nothing in the redistribution: the blows to his body and his ego impose their own marks but he receives no compensation. It is only as member of the team, identifying his interests with those of the team, that he is compensated by the imposed punishment.

In cases where the referee judges that the foul warrants a yellow or even a red card as well as a penalty, then the offender himself also suffers a deprivation in the punishment. Removed from the game, or threatened with suspension for a subsequent game, the player's own interests are negatively affected in the punishment, as well as the impact on the interests of the team, in which he too has a share. But even in this case the victim of the foul does not benefit or experience any redress to counterbalance the pain or loss he personally had suffered beyond perhaps the satisfaction of seeing that a deliberate or vicious foul had been recognised as such by the referee and that the perpetrator did not get away with it.

CORRECTION AND RESTORATION COMPARED

Punishment in this restorative case also has a pedagogical moment.[12] The player or the team that resorted to unlawful actions in pursuit of their interests should learn from the experience of the penalty, which substituted an almost certain goal for a probable goal, that crime does not pay. But the learning involved is different to that in the corrective case. The players and teams are not like children who are learning the proper way to behave: they are (presumed to be) already in a position to know the rules and the reasons for the rules, and to know the consequences of infringements. That they in fact learn from the imposition of the punishment is not the main point of the punishment. Rather, the main point is that the balance of fairness in the game be restored.

THE COMMON GOOD AND PUNISHMENT

This analysis of restorative punishment is only plausible if we take for granted a number of assumptions, some of which are made explicit above. First, there is the assumption that a basic equality is guaranteed by the fact that teams compete in the game under the same conditions and rules. Second, there is the assumption that players in a team are united in sharing the interests of the team, and that their interests as players are identified with those of the team. It is this second assumption that enables people to accept the fairness of restorative punishments from which they personally do not benefit, even though they had been personally wronged in the foul. Training in sportsmanship and the discipline which forms character enables people to see their own interests in this way. We tend to make these assumptions easily since they are part of what we take for granted in games. But, although they are easily made, the assumptions are very important. Both of these assumptions touch on what I want to call the common good of social existence. The second assumption refers to the common good of players united in a team. Team members cooperate with one another and make their individual contributions for the sake of something at which they all aim, namely, victory in the game, the tournament, the league, the cup. It is the team's interests which are at stake in unlawful behaviour, and it is the team's interests which are restored in punishment. By contrast, the first assumption refers to the common good of teams who are opposed to one another as competitors in a sport. All who participate in a given sport value the maintenance of standards of fairness guaranteed by rules and sanctions; although their interests as competitors are mutually opposed, they share a common interest in maintaining fair conditions of competition.

OTHER MODELS OF PUNISHMENT

In undertaking to investigate the origins of our ideas of punishment, I listed various models which would have to be considered, namely, the corrective, the restorative, and others from the margins of social existence. I have discussed the corrective and restorative models which are taken from familiar situations in our lives, the rearing of children and participation in sport. The comparison of these proved useful in relation to specifying a common good in punishment. It now remains to consider other models of punishment. There are models which are based on experience of life at the margins of society, and while I presume not everyone has direct experience of such situations, the relevant vicarious experience is available to all. From our exposure to fiction and film we are familiar with the typical images of life on the margins of social existence, whether at the stage of the establishment of social order or at the stage of its disintegration. Examples are stories of the frontier Wild West (Clint Eastwood in *Outlaw Josey Wales*) or stories from the urban jungle (Charles Bronson and *Death Wish*).

The Western examples are familiar. Settlers are making a life for themselves in parts of the world which have not known civilisation. The west or any other frontier in that sense is wild. As yet there is no society, no law or institutions of law enforcement. Individuals struggle to make a home for themselves in an inhospitable environment, being able to rely only on their own skill and resources. The baddies, and there are always such, for otherwise there would be no story, have some extra strength or resources which give them the chance of taking advantage of the weaker. They rustle their cattle, take advantage of their womenfolk, steal their money, break down their fences, and even kill. The hero of the story stands up to the bad guy, pursues him and in the eventual showdown proves himself to be stronger or more skilful. He then sees to it that the bad guy gets what is coming to him – death, imprisonment or exile.

In this typical story, the wrongdoing of the bad guy is at the expense of some individual and his family; there is a definite victim, and it is on behalf of this victim that the hero acts. Society and its institutions are still in the process of being built, so that society itself only features in the story in a shadowy way, perhaps as something to be realised in the future – hence the frequent recurrence of the line about the life we want to make for our children. Notice this for instance in stories in which the hero takes on the office of sheriff or marshal and sees to it that law is established in town. But for the present the hero imposes a punishment on behalf of the victim.

More recent film scripts depict the chaos at the margins of society where law and order has broken down, where the usual institutions of law and punishment are no longer effective. Unable to rely on society for protection, the victim of urban or organised crime looks to the self-appointed vigilante or executioner, as typified in the series of films entitled *Death Wish* with Charles Bronson. The audience buys into the agenda of the protector, because the victim's desire for vindication and protection and the demand that the wrongdoers not get away with their crime are genuine aspects of the human hunger for justice.

These models from the margins of social existence, whether from the steps in the creation of social order or from the steps in the disintegration of social order, are sometimes relied upon to make sense of our practice of punishment and of our language to speak of it. This approach is typical of individualist political theories, which would see social existence as an artificial construct for the purpose of securing the interests of individuals. These theories usually imagine a scenario apart from society, frequently labelled the state of nature, and ask what reasons individuals might have for joining with others in society. This question seeks the reasons individuals might have in subjecting themselves to an authority which would have the power to make laws and to punish lawbreaking. The kinds of reasons which are typically considered are confined to descriptions of the interests of individuals, as for instance, the individual's need for security against others (Thomas Hobbes), the individual's need for the protection of basic rights to life, liberty and property (John Locke), or the individual's desire to be free (Jean Jacques Rousseau). Frequently enough, discussions devoted to the rationale of punishment presuppose such political philosophies. Punishment is understood in terms of the interests of the wronged individual, the victim. Punishment is part of arrangements to afford the victim some security in a situation which would otherwise be most insecure – this is Hobbes's version; or punishment is part of arrangements to vindicate the rights of the victim who had been wronged, and to afford him a secure space defined by his rights – this is Locke's version. However, if we rely on these models to explain human society and institutions like punishment, there is a real danger that we will generate a one-sided if not biased view, because of the tendency to overlook the engendering context of the model, namely the absence or disintegration of social order.

Because there is no society, no communality between wrong-doer and victim in this scenario, the concept of the common good does not arise in this description of punishment. It is purely a matter of how individuals relate to one another in a conflicted situation in which one by virtue of greater strength or skill is a threat to the other. An objection could be raised at this point to the effect that any attempt to punish must presuppose a common good in some minimal sense. Punishment as the deprivation of some of the punishee's good, liberty, money, company or indeed life presupposes that both parties recognise and value the good at stake: otherwise the intention of punishment could not occur or be understood. While I

concede this point, I do not accept it as an objection to my
argument. While there is indeed a recognition and valuing of
the same goods by both parties, there is not necessarily a
cooperation in pursuit of the same good, or a pursuit by one
of a good for the other. This latter would only arise on the
basis of a restoration model.

MODELS APPLIED TO SOCIAL EXPERIENCE

Can we rely on the models of correction and restoration to
speak of the actual institutions and practices of punishment
in our society? Frequently enough we find echoes of these
models, as people make reference to rehabilitation and paying
a debt. Perhaps in the past, when there was a greater level of
consensus on moral and public standards, such references were
unproblematic. Now however, there are definite problems. Let
us consider first the question whether penalties imposed for
crime in society can be understood by comparison with
penalties imposed in a game for infringement of the rules.

Is social life like a game? There are definite advantages in
thinking that it is. For instance, in a game one can presume
on the two levels of common good referred to above; those
who are in competition with one another agree on the maintenance of the terms and conditions of their conflict, and those
who cooperate on the same team are united in pursuit of their
common good of victory. The rules make sense in relation to
these goods, and on occasion the rules will be modified so
that the common good might better be achieved. Now there
is an obvious advantage in thinking of the laws of society in
similar terms. Just as with the participants in sport one can
assume that participants in social life share a common good;
even if they are in conflict with one another, if their interests
are mutually opposed, they can be presumed to agree and to
cooperate in maintaining and operating the laws and institutions which regulate their conflict. The analogy with the
game makes clear just how much this is assumed and taken
for granted. It does not have to be made explicit or argued
for. This is the point I want to emphasise: how much can be
taken for granted, and how much people do take for granted

when the model they use for understanding society is that of the game: 'we are all in this together', 'you have to abide by the rules', 'the rules are there for everyone'.

There are also disadvantages in using the game-restoration model. These arise because of the difficulties involved in using a situation which is merely a part of social life to model the whole. We experience sport and games as only a part of our life, while the whole of our life is social and subject to the law. One can decide to opt out of a game or withdraw from a sport altogether, but there is no similar option available in relation to our social existence. One might become an exile or refugee but that is simply to have moved from one social situation to another.

Furthermore, the assumption of communality and a balance of benefits and burdens may be challenged in the case of a particular society. I have been contrasting two kinds of models: one kind which assumes a communality between punisher and punishee, offender and victim, a common good of all participants, and another which assumes an opposition between punisher and punishee, offender and victim. In the latter case, society is under threat, precarious, in need of defence against disruptive elements.

There are those at this point who would argue: which model we choose to use will depend on how we describe the situation we are facing. And they might argue further that the opposition model is the appropriate one to use because the crime we are experiencing is not simply the misbehaviour of those who are still being educated into correct social performance, or the opportunistic rule breaking of those who still want to play the game. Rather, crime in modern society, with the elements of organisation, international connections especially involving drugs, and sophisticated white-collar crime due to technological opportunities, involves a direct threat to society itself; therefore the appropriate categories are those of defence, and indeed, even of civil war. This particular response appeals to an interpretation of experience, and so appears to be empirical, in describing the way things are. The practical implications for penal policy of this empirical reading are clear.

There is no balance to be restored: those who threaten society and its members are outside of society, and they must be dealt with, for the sake of society and its members. The good of the punishee is not a factor.

A similar empirical story can lead to alternative practical implications however. For instance others might well concede that the crime situation at present reflects more a civil war situation than the rule breaking of players in the same game. There is a high correlation of crime with social and economic deprivation; this reflects a situation in which a third of the population is excluded from sharing in the benefits of social cooperation and increased prosperity. Crime is to a large extent the response of those who are effectively excluded from society. The civil war category is not inappropriate. But instead of concluding to a corresponding appropriate form of penal policy, the proponents of this argument might focus on the dynamic of exclusion (and indeed on penal policy as an implement of that exclusion) and instead of accepting what is happening, protest that it should be different. There should be no exclusion: concern for all the members and elements of society requires that exclusionary tendencies be resisted and all be allowed share in the common wealth. And so the language and practice of punishment should aim at sustaining and repairing the balance between all the members of the one society.

The possibility of this particular move in the argument underlines for us the point that the choice of the basic model is not determined by the facts. It is not simply a matter of observing what is going on and choosing the correct remedy. It is not like being faced with a fire and having to choose the correct fire extinguisher: foam or water? Is there electricity involved? Then foam! It is more like recognising that it is necessary also to ask why there is a fire and what is burning, and to try to remove the cause of the fire. And so which punishment model is appropriate: one which presumes a common good or one which is antagonistic? If there is social conflict then perhaps the antagonistic one; but why is there social conflict, and would the adoption of the antagonistic model make that conflict worse?

I have sketched a polarity between two kinds of models, one presuming a common good, and the other presuming antagonism without a common good. These models generate opposed views of the role of the state with its various arms (legislative, judicial, executive) in relation to punishment. Following the polarity I have sketched, we can regard the state in either of two ways: either as an agent for the victim acting against the criminal or as an agent for the common good responding to wrongdoing.[13] In the latter case, it is not possible to say 'acting against the criminal', since the disjunction between criminal and victim is not mirrored in a corresponding disjunction between criminal and the common good. The common good must be a good also for the criminal. Of course, if the state, in claiming to act for the common good, does not address the good of the victims and of potential victims, and does not act so as to sustain a high level of confidence in the law and its officers, then its claims will be seen to be hollow. The growing voice on behalf of victims is warranted. But it has its dangers. The main danger is that we abandon a model presuming a common good between punisher and punishee, victim and criminal, in favour of a model which sees these roles only as antagonistic.

The shift from the view of the state as agent for the common good to seeing the state as agent for the victim is understandable. But it is also dangerous. That justice be done for victims is an element of the common good, but to give it the central role is liable to undermine the comprehensive common good. To omit it is also dangerous, leading to a loss of respect for law and its institutions, and to an undermining of trust in the state and in the protection it offers. The growing tendency to see punishment primarily or exclusively as a matter of the relationship between the victim and the perpetrator of crime both reflects and contributes to a disintegration of social order in which members share a common good, however minimal.

CONCLUSION

In this chapter I have identified as my topic the language available at both the reflective and common-sense levels for speaking about cooperation. I have taken an example from the literature on punishment to illustrate the concern about the self-understandings of those involved in operating the penal system. A range of possible working credos was outlined. Those who cooperate in running the institutions of the criminal justice system, and indeed any of our state institutions, must be able to make some sense of what they are doing in order to be able to operate effectively. And the content of the particular working credo they rely on will condition what actually occurs in the interaction with offenders or clients. In a further step I contrasted the assumptions behind two types of models of punishment, those which assumed some communality between punisher and punished, and those which assumed a fundamental antagonism between them. In the first type of model, some common good shared by the different parties is presupposed. I argued further that the assumption of a common good would condition the type of explanation of punishment adopted, and correspondingly the type of working credo which might be possible for practitioners. It is clear, for instance, that the caring credo identified and preferred by Rutherford reflects an acknowledgement of the common humanity of offenders and the officials of the penal system. The commitment to fairness and decency in the treatment of offenders is based on a recognition of goods which are common to all, whatever side of the punishment divide they are on.

On the other hand, I argued that the adoption of explanatory models of punishment predicated on antagonism without a common good would contribute to the further disintegration of social cohesion which in turn would make crime more likely. The discussion of punishment in terms of working credos and the common good provided me with an illustration of the argument of the opening paragraphs. There I considered the relationship between the analyses of reflective scientists and the self-understandings of people engaged in everyday activities. What practitioners within the penal system understand themselves to be doing is conditioned to some extent by the language available to them from the theoretical analyses of experts. Hence the importance of reflecting on the language of analysis with a view to improving the possibilities of social action. The discussion also opens up issues which must be clarified further in the following chapters. In dealing with punishment I introduced the notion of models; it will be necessary to investigate models of rationality in some detail, to substantiate the claims that some models are deficient in relation to our explanation of cooperation, and to indicate the route of development towards more adequate models.

CHAPTER 2

AN ALTERNATIVE RATIONALITY

In the first chapter I distinguished between the spontaneous, common-sense answers which anyone might give to questions like 'what are you doing? why are you doing that?', and the explanations for the same activities which are produced by the appropriate sciences of economics, sociology, politics and anthropology. This distinction between ordinary speech and the technical models of human science is relevant because I am investigating the language available for understanding cooperation. I took Rousseau's scenario of someone in need provoking contrasting responses as a starting point. Coming to the aid of someone in need is indeed a case of human cooperation, but it is an extreme example and cannot stand for the full range of cases. However, it does serve the function of allowing us to challenge the prevalent assumption that all cooperation is motivated by self-interest.

I now want to consider further the polarisation which this extreme example provokes. For this purpose I will reflect on a statement about the common good made by Pope John Paul II in his encyclical letter on social concern, *Sollicitudo Rei Socialis*. The Pope speaks of solidarity. Solidarity, he says,

> . . . is not a feeling of vague compassion or shallow distress at the misfortunes of so many people, both near and far. On the contrary, it is a firm and persevering determination to commit oneself to the common good; that is to say to the good of all and of each individual, because we are all really responsible for all.[1]

The meaning of the statement seems clear enough. Everyone is said to be responsible for everyone else, and this requires of each person a moral response which consists in a firm commitment to the common good. Not 'every man for himself' but 'everyone for everyone else'.

But if the meaning is clear, is the conclusion drawn acceptable? Imagine the responses it would evoke: 'why should anyone take responsibility for others, and bear extra costs and burdens which benefit them, not herself?', 'why should I have to pay to support people who do nothing for me?' Translate this prescription into the debates on contemporary problems: world hunger, the destruction of the rainforests, the environment, the North–South divide, unemployment, the burden of debt. Can the Pope seriously expect all involved to take responsibility for everyone else? Hasn't each person enough to do to look out for herself, and hasn't each state enough to do in safeguarding its own interests?

Talk of the common good is likely to meet with a challenge in terms of the individual questioner's good. The challenge takes it for granted that there is no problem in the individual identifying her own good and making it the purpose of action. But to take as the purpose of one's action, the good of others, or of some unnamed communality, without reference to one's own good, is startling. Why would anyone do it? And even more radically, why should anyone do it? The question is posed dramatically in Joseph Heller's novel, *Catch-22*. 'Catch-22' was the impossibility of being released from active service in the US Air Force on psychiatric grounds even though the rule book said the only way one could be released was on psychiatric grounds. Yossarian, the hero of the book, applied for release on the grounds that he was going crazy, and his request was refused, because he was obviously sane enough to recognise that he was going mad and therefore wasn't insane. If he were mad, he wouldn't apply for release: he would continue to fight.[2]

> There was only one catch and that was Catch-22, which specified that a concern for one's own safety in the face of dangers that were real and immediate was the process of a rational mind. Orr was crazy and could be grounded. All he had to do was ask; and

as soon as he did, he would no longer be crazy and would have to fly more missions. Orr would be crazy to fly more missions and sane if he didn't, but if he was sane he had to fly them. If he flew them he was crazy and didn't have to; but if he didn't want to he was sane and had to.

Continuing his efforts to get released, Yossarian pointed out to his superior officer, Major Major, that he didn't want to fly any more missions against the enemy, since they were obviously trying to kill him. The officer was at a loss how to reply.

> *What could you do?* Major Major asked himself again. What could you do with a man who looked you squarely in the eye and said he would rather die than be killed in combat . . .
> 'Would you like to see our country lose?' Major Major asked.
> 'We won't lose. We've got more men, more money and more material. There are ten million men in uniform who could replace me. Some people are getting killed and a lot more are making money and having fun. Let somebody else get killed.'
> 'But suppose everybody on our side felt that way.'
> 'Then I'd certainly be a damned fool to feel any other way. Wouldn't I?'
> *What could you possibly say to him?*

The officer's final challenge that Yossarian should consider the consequences of everyone thinking the way he did fails miserably. There would certainly be no point in a single soldier risking his own life if none of the rest of the army was willing to do so too.

What if everyone refused to bear their share of the burden of common effort? Then indeed, there could be no common effort. But equally, any one individual would be foolish to think that she alone could carry the whole operation. Contemporary political and practical philosophy takes very seriously the analysis of such scenarios. One cannot speak of the common good today and hope to make sense of it unless one can deal with the question which many pose to the common good tradition: 'why should I bear a disproportionate share of the burden of some common effort, from which I personally derive no benefit?'

THE RATIONALITY OF SELF-INTEREST

A question like this seeks a reason which can give the questioner grounds for cooperation, that is, some argument which is taken as conclusive and which evokes appropriate action based on conviction. But what would qualify as a reason? That depends on the mind-set of the questioner. For instance, I might start from the presupposition that the rationality of action depends on the role of that action in relation to the interests of the actor, such that if the action achieves those interests, brings about some goal held by the actor, then it is rational, but if it does not serve the interests of the actor, then it is irrational. In that case, only the kind of reason which can show some proposed action to be in the interests of the addressee will be acceptable. Let us go back to the basic question: 'why should I bear a disproportionate share of the burden of some common effort, from which I personally derive no benefit?' Let us allow for the sake of argument the presupposition that the benefits to the questioner are negligible, relative to the costs. In this case, there is no answer to the question which would be rational in the sense of rationality outlined above. So it is clear that a narrow specification of rationality already determines whether or not an answer to the question raised is possible. In the following sections I will be exploring the model of rationality which underlies much of the theory in economics and other human sciences. I hope to be able to show that adoption of that model as the basis of scientific explanation renders irrational much activity which healthy common sense can accept as meaningful. And furthermore, to the extent that the theory leads to the adoption of particular strategies, that it is likely to result in the exclusion of perfectly rational courses of action. The point is, they would be rational in some sense not recognised by the model.

THE 'PRISONERS' DILEMMA'

There is a considerable body of opinion today questioning the wisdom of the established model of rationality which is so influential in economics. Within philosophy the discussion of this question frequently relies on games theory. Games are situations in which there are (1) two or more rational agents with a choice of strategies, (2) an outcome which is the combined result of the strategy of each agent, and (3) a pay-off to each agent measured by the value of the outcome to each. Each agent is presumed to seek to maximise the pay-off to himself through a rational choice of strategy. This assumption incorporates in the analysis the aspects of self-interest distinctive of the dominant perspective discussed above. The 'prisoner's dilemma' is one such game.

> Two prisoners are each held by the police, who know that they have committed a serious crime, but cannot secure conviction against either unless at least one of them confesses. The police, however, have sufficient evidence to secure a conviction against each of them on a minor charge of income-tax evasion. The police offer to each prisoner separately the following deal: if that prisoner will confess while the other does not, the police will not press either the major or the minor charge, and he will go scot-free. If he does not confess, while the other prisoner does, the police will secure his conviction on both charges, and he will get ten years. If both prisoners confess, the court will give them five years each. However, if neither confesses, each will get one year for income-tax evasion.[3]

What is the rational strategy? The explanatory model of the rational chooser assumes that the chooser will consult only his own interests, and will choose so as to maximise utility to himself. On this assumption then, each one must choose between two pairs: [1 or 10] and [0 or 5]. There is a pair, because no chooser knows what the other will decide, but at the same time must take into consideration the implications of the other's choice. The option of remaining silent will lead to one of two outcomes, depending on whether the other also remains silent or confesses. But what the other will do is unknown. Each must consider his own option in terms of remaining silent or confessing. Looking at it this way, each chooses between two packages with a low and a high figure in each package [1 or 10] and [0 or 5]. The latter package is obviously preferable since both its low and its high figures are better than the alternative pair of low and high scores: no jail beats one year, and five years' jail beats ten. For the individual deciding in isolation in terms of his own interests, the preference is clear: the rational thing to do is to confess, regardless of what the other does!

The significant word here is *isolation*, and that is why this scenario is referred to as the prisoners' dilemma, even when the details of the choice have nothing to do with jail sentences. The prisoners are in separate cells, isolated, unable to communicate with one another. So if the prisoners did have the chance of coordinating their choices, they might be able to view their options in a new way. Instead of looking only at their individual interests, they could also look at the advantages of cooperation. If they would both keep silent, they would have to spend one year each in jail, so this course of action is to be compared with the other combinations of sentences: [1 + 1], [0 + 10], and [5 + 5]. The total of two years is obviously preferable to the other total of ten. But would this cooperative option not be foolish for the individual, given that he has a chance of getting off scot-free? Is he choosing 1 over 0? However, it is only a chance of 0, a possibility, since any prisoner choosing in isolation, who realises that his rational course of action is to confess, would also have to calculate that the other will be equally rational and self-interested, and will also confess, so that the most probable outcome of self-interested choices made in isolation is five years each. Therefore the cooperative strategy of both keeping silent leads to an outcome [1 + 1], which is to be compared to the cumulative outcome of isolated strategies to confess of [5 + 5]. For the individual, if he can trust his partner, the advantages of keeping silent are overwhelming: one year's jail beats five.

If he can trust his partner. Because of course a defection by his partner will land him with ten years in jail, and the other will get off scot-free. The temptation to defect is ever present because its pay-off is unmistakeable: one year in jail may be preferable to five, but for any individual, no jail is very much preferable to a little jail.

The advantages of cooperation are considerable. But

equally, its dangers have become apparent. It is precisely the existence of the agreement and the assurance that the other will keep his word that gives the individual prisoner the opportunity of benefiting by defection. Because I now have a reasonable expectation of what the other will do I can rearrange my options to get the best for myself. But recognising that the same applies to the other, I have to acknowledge my new vulnerability. The basic question above, 'why should I bear a disproportionate share of the burden of some common effort, from which I personally derive no benefit?', can now be given a new formulation in the light of the prisoners' dilemma: 'why should I make myself vulnerable to defection by others, rather than defecting myself?', 'why should I risk being a sucker, when I might be a cheat?'

CURRENT ISSUES

Translate this question into the issues confronting us today, for example responsibility for the environment and responsibility for the well-being of the workforce. Take environmental issues. The threatened extinction of some species and the excessive depletion of some stocks make agreement and cooperation at the international level necessary in order to deal with the problem. In Europe especially we see the tension between local and even national interests on the one hand, and the international handling of the problem on the other. Fish quotas are imposed in order to prevent over-fishing and allow fish stocks to recover. Look at such a dilemma from the perspective of a single Irish trawler or fishing port: if the other nations and groups fishing the North Atlantic do not cut back, then it is pointless for the Irish fleet to implement quotas, since one small section cutting back will hardly impinge on the problem. On the other hand, if everyone else does cut back, then it will not make any difference to the overall situation if one small section of the industry exceeds the quota. From the perspective of the individual participant in such cooperative measures, it is never in one's own interest to abide by restrictions. What is in one's interest is that there should be some regulation protecting stocks, that all other participants should abide by this regulation, and that one's own defection should remain undetected.

Fish quotas, milk production quotas, these and such like are the business of contemporary politics and daily news reports, and it is in terms of examples such as these that the notion of the common good has to be elucidated. Other examples from the world of industry illustrate the same point. Efforts to improve the working conditions of employees (for example noise reduction, protection against toxic materials), along with the control of pollution, figure as costs in the economy of the firm. These are extra production costs, which do not promise direct returns. (Leave aside for a moment issues like the cost of workdays lost due to illness, the cost of bad product image due to negative publicity.) As such, they provide us with further concrete examples of the original question, why anyone should bear a disproportionate share of the costs of joint ventures. Why should any firm take on extra costs for which it cannot expect to receive corresponding benefits? As employers are only too quick to point out, extra costs make firms less competitive, and any firm which goes it alone in adopting such measures in a competitive environment is going to lose out. Its interests will suffer. Only if all competitors conform and take on board the extra costs would it be rational in terms of self-interest for a single participant to do so. But then, if all competitors were so public-spirited, any one participant would be in a position to exploit their vulnerability by avoiding these costs. It would be rational, relative to the interests of the individual herself, to defect, if she could get away with it undetected.

These examples highlight what has been called 'the tragedy of the commons' by biologist Garrett Hardin.[4] Everyone has an interest in everyone else keeping the rules and they alone breaking them. That is the extent to which social existence – conformity to rules – can be justified, within the rationality of calculating self-interest. It never makes sense for one individual to act so as to safeguard the common assets: if nobody else does, it makes no difference and one loses out; if everybody else does, then one person defaulting makes no difference to the overall problem. From any individual's point of view, the rational strategy is to default, if she can get away with it. The rationality of individuals pursuing their own interest leads to the destruction or loss of the common resources on which all ultimately depend, so all lose out eventually.

RATIONALITY EXAMINED

Martin Hollis is a philosopher who has been studying our models of rationality for several decades now. A significant book he wrote along with E. Nell in 1975 bore the title *Rational Economic Man.*[5] In a more recent book, *The Cunning of Reason*, he raises again the issue of the model of rationality in economic theory.[6] He identifies the anomaly we noted above in discussing the prisoners' dilemma, namely, that it is the existence of trust and cooperation which gives any individual the possibility of breaking that trust to her own advantage. From the perspective of individual interest, the perspective of the *homo economicus*, it is never the rational strategy to cooperate so as to achieve the better cumulative outcome. The individual is always advised to defect.

Of course the prisoners' dilemma is deliberately constructed to model one aspect of social interaction. It is suggested that this aspect is typical of much social interaction in modern societies. The other on whose cooperation one relies is a stranger, and one has no basis for trusting the stranger except to the extent that her own interests are involved. Choosing the strategy for action only on the basis of one's interests, there will always be the temptation to exploit the cooperation of others. Generalising this analysis of the prisoners' dilemma, Hollis shows that, according to the rationality of self-interest, each actor has a dominant reason to defect. Calculating in terms of maximising the pay-off to oneself, each prefers to benefit without cost, to having to bear the cost.

Take the day-tripper users of a beautiful beach. Each wants to find a clean beach when they arrive. However, to tidy up one's own litter and refuse is a cost at the end of the day, for which there is no direct return. The beach users have no interest in the state of the beach on the following day. What reason would they have, in terms of the assumptions of self-interest, calculating the maximisation of pay-off to themselves? On those assumptions, it seems they would have no reason to clean up, and would leave a littered beach! The result of each one calculating only in terms of their own interests is that together they bring about an outcome which is unattractive to all of them. A preferred outcome, namely, a clean beach, is within their reach, but they cannot achieve it as long as they are calculating in terms of self-interest and also assuming that everyone else is also calculating in the same way. This last remark is crucial, because a clean beach is not achievable by one person acting alone. There must be cooperation, even if it is not coordinated. But if my model of rationality leads me to expect that the others are not going to bear unrewarded costs, then I am reinforced in my reluctance to do so myself.

Hollis shows how this conclusion is inescapable, within the terms of the model of the rational economic agent. The rational economic agent who seeks to maximise utility in the sense of benefits in relation to costs has a *dominant reason* to defect. The same will be true for each and every agent. So if this conclusion is generalised to any number of players, they will be found to generate an outcome inferior for all of them, despite the fact that there was a possible outcome better for all, which all recognise as such. They will end up with their third preference, despite the fact that the second preference was possible. And so each of the prisoners in the scenario depicted above gets five years in jail (third preference), even though an outcome of one year each was achievable (second preference), and only because each is tempted to try for release at the expense of the other (first preference). Similarly the visitors to the beach leave it littered, even though it would have been possible with a little effort to keep it tidy, because each is tempted by the possibility of having the benefit without the work and is put off by the possibility of being a sucker, doing more than their fair share of the work.

The same problem is evidenced in what is called the free-rider paradox. In Germany one can buy a newspaper by taking one from a stand and putting the money in a box. The system relies on trust. If everyone cooperates with the system, all benefit by having a convenient access to the daily papers. But suppose that each *most* prefers to take the paper for nothing, while others pay, and *least* prefers that he pays while others get it free. Then each has a dominant reason not to pay. The paper stands are withdrawn and the free-riders lose their papers, through their own self-defeating choices. Extrapolate the argument to the problems mentioned above, of the economic and environmental problems facing us. It seems then that rational agents will fail to save water voluntarily in droughts, will fail to hold back on closures which ruin local communities, will buy the cheaper bread which results in the closure of local bakeries, will travel to the suburban shopping centres which results in the degradation of the town and city centres, and will fail to conserve the stocks of fish on which their livelihood depends. These are typical cases exhibiting the fatal preference order which leads all to defeat their second-best outcome by contributing to their third-best.

This is the problem which lies at the basis of the attempts in the history of political philosophy to explain the reasonableness of society and the rational grounds of obligation. The problem is a problem precisely because one starts with the model of the rational agent as someone pursuing her own interests. How is one to make sense of costly cooperation? There is no difficulty with situations in which the return to oneself for contributions to a common project are immediate and predictable. But there is a real difficulty with social situations in which the free-rider problem is an element, that is, where there is the possibility of one doing all the work while the other bums a ride. The seventeenth-century English political philosopher, Thomas Hobbes, described the problem clearly in his book *Leviathan*: all prefer peace but will inevitably be at war with one another. And even if they see the trap and try to avoid it by setting up a contract, by agreeing to keep the peace, they are still damned to a state of war. The problem is that the contract only reproduces the question: will any agent keep the contract or not? Each has a reason in terms of her own interests to defect, and the contract collapses. Hobbes offers the solution of coercion. The existence of a coercive power which enforces the contract would provide people with additional considerations when calculating the balance of burdens and benefits. The likelihood of being fined for littering would change the calculation and result in different behaviour by visitors to the beach. Reliance on effective policing will give people reason for expecting others to contribute to a clean beach and so enable one to cooperate without the fear of being a sucker. But if Hobbes's solution is correct, it means that rational agents cannot rely on their rationality to solve their problems but must rely on coercive norms. What is more, when policing is only nominal and the likelihood of being caught is minimalised, rational calculation in terms of costs and benefits prompts one to consider the advantages of breaking the law. Then the rationality of self-interest can appear to undermine compliance in social co-operation.

Hollis's analysis reveals the seeming irrationality and self-destructiveness of our economic exploitation of our environment, the reshaping of our communities and the total redefinition of the quality of life. Is it not ridiculous that on our dominant model of rationality in the most successful of our human sciences and indeed in the modern tradition of liberal political philosophy, it is not rational to do what every-one can recognise is best?[7]

Hollis argues that a fundamental element in the setting of the problem is the understanding of human motivation and reason operative in the dominant model. This understanding owes a lot to David Hume, and the distinction between desire and beliefs or reason. Indeed, much of Hume's moral and political philosophy was anticipated by Hobbes, as J. L. Mackie points out.[8] On this view, reason is slave of the passions, an instrument to enable one achieve what one desires. Desires are arbitrary and merely given. As long as this is the under-standing of the human person in human science the problem remains, because, by definition, one cannot have a reason for changing desires and preferences. Humeans cannot admit of a desire to do the rational thing. What is needed according to

Hollis is an amendment of the analysis of rational agency so that an agent can be understood to take her own preferences as a reason for her choice, when she knows that others have similar preference rankings. The agent's knowledge of her own preferences and a reasonable expectation of how others will act need to be made factors in the analysis of her decision making. Then it is conceivable that action proceeds not just from desire but also from beliefs and convictions. In contrast to the Humean axiom, belief can be taken to be a possible motive to the will. So rational agents might act from objectively good reasons. This involves a move from a Humean account of desire and reason where reason is slave of the passions to a Kantian view which accepts that one can have interests conceptually independent of desires.

With this alternative understanding of the relationship of reason and desire it would be possible to solve the problem identified by Hobbes and analysed by Hollis. From his analysis Hollis identified as the Leviathan trap the dominance of the reason to choose to defect, even though it led to a less preferred outcome. The trap was unavoidable in some situations of social cooperation as long as human action was to be understood as driven by the satisfaction of self-interest. But now the agent can be considered to have an external reason to choose to cooperate if she can be moved by the knowledge of an alternative outcome and the belief that it is better. There are two conditions for this: first, her belief is true, that is, there is a better outcome. But this conclusion requires on the side both of the agent and of the observer a more encompassing point of view than self-interest. The situation must be viewed in terms like fairness or justice, what leads to overall happiness, or what is in the common good. The second condition is that she can expect the other player also to accept the external reason and draw the same conclusion, namely that there is an alternative and better outcome.

This amounts to saying that the solution to the trap lies in trust, which is not founded in self-interest, whether of the long-term variety or the immediate variety in the fear of punishment. Hollis concludes that to defeat the Leviathan trap both in theory and in reality we need trust in the moral sense. This means reliance on a norm which is neither consensual (rowers rowing in stroke) nor coercive (backed up by threat of punishment) but moral.[9] That is, one has to be able to expect a certain kind of behaviour from others not because it is in their own interests, but because it is the right thing to do. One has to have a basis for asking neighbours on the beach to dispose of their litter and there has to be a basis of complaint when they fail to do so.

Talk of the common good points to duties of citizens and states to favour the common good over their own interests. Such talk seems totally impracticable to those who understand economic and political reality in terms of a model of practical rationality based on individual interest. But now it appears that *that* model itself is suspect. As the analysis has shown, one whose thinking and action conform to the model is trapped. Such a rational agent is condemned to choosing a worse outcome than is necessary; if we followed the advice based on this rationality we would end up with our third preferred outcome even though the second would be achievable. In the name of rationality we are engaged in a self-defeating and frustrating adventure. Hollis's analysis points to the need for an adjustment of the basic model of rationality on which we rely for our explanations and prescriptions in social affairs. In the following chapters I will investigate possible ways in which the limitations of a model predicated exclusively on self-interest can be overcome. Chapter 3 considers the notion of altruism as a solution and Chapter 4 reflects on the common good which unites people in small-scale cooperative ventures.

PRACTICE AND THEORY

Before proceeding with the investigation, however, it is worth our while to return to the questions raised in Chapter 1. There I distinguished between the thinking of people involved in social life and the theoretical modelling of that thinking within the human sciences which explain social phenomena. I asked about the relationship between these two. The discussion of Hollis's analysis in this chapter provides us with a treatment of one influential model of rationality which is relied upon by the science of economics. The criticism which Hollis brings to bear is not primarily to remark that the thinking presented in the model is not the way in which people actually think. Rather, his criticism consists in highlighting the problems and traps which are likely to arise when one is restricted to a rationality of self-interest. The problems and traps are not simply those which arise within the theory. They are also problems for people actually involved in social interaction who plan their own interventions in the light of what they expect other people to do. What those expectations are will depend significantly on what people consider to be rational behaviour. If their model of rationality is that of maximising self-interest, then the 'tragedy of the commons' is likely to be a recurrent feature of social life. That is, individuals pursuing their own interests will lead to the destruction of common assets on which all ultimately depend. Recalling the distinction between the thinking of people in actual social situations and the modelling of that thinking in human sciences, Hollis's discussion allows us to see that these cannot be completely separated. There is an obvious sense in which the scientific model merely systematises what is to be found in ordinary experience. But the relation between the two is not simply that of ordinary participant and scientific observer. What the scientists articulate as rational feeds into the expectations of social actors, since each one plans her interventions in the light of expectations of what others will do. People's expectations are conditioned by experts' forecasts.[10] Furthermore, recalling the distinction between description and prescription, Hollis's analysis also allows us to see how a supposedly descriptive science can have a prescriptive effect. While merely offering an analysis of what goes on, scientific observers nonetheless shape the language in which people argue for what they want to bring about, and they shape the expectations of what others will want and will do.

My objective in this book is to explore the language of the common good and its associated model of rationality as suitable for analysing and justifying social cooperation. While the above two distinctions, namely, that between description and prescription, and that between social participant and scientific observer, will always be useful in relation to discussion of social reality, it is clear that they do not reflect strict separations. The language of the common good must be such that it can perform both descriptive and prescriptive functions, and that it can be of use in the thinking of social participants and in the analysis of scientific observers.

CHAPTER 3

IS ALTRUISM THE KEY TO THE COMMON GOOD?

The search for a model of practical rationality which is free of the limitations conditioned by the assumption of self-interest has led many in the direction of altruism. A recent collection of essays entitled *Altruism*, edited by Ellen Frankel Paul and others, is typical of a widespread contemporary interest in the topic.[1] The philosophical interest in altruism derives from the need to find solutions to problems similar to those outlined in the previous chapter. Those problems arise because of the limitations of instrumental self-interest in explaining cooperation. It is doubtful, however, whether the solution can be provided by the notion of altruism. The required alternative to egoism is not its opposite, altruism, but a practical philosophy which is freed of the disjunction egoism–altruism. It is important at this point to note the danger of confusion between two levels, that of theory and that of what is implicit in activity. I want to discuss altruism as a doctrine at the level of theory, which is developed to make sense of other-directed action. The difficulty is that the word is commonly used simply to name other-directed action – altruistic behaviour – without presuming any particular explanatory model. Of course I recognise the occurrence of other-directed activity, and indeed I want to encourage and facilitate such activity by articulating an adequate explanatory model. In this chapter however, my main focus is on showing the inadequacy of altruism as an explanatory model. I will

44

argue that its main weakness is that it retains assumptions linked to the disjunction of egoism and altruism. One danger with altruism is that it emphasises the separateness of the other who benefits from the person acting. Is it possible to have an explanatory model which recognises the communality rather than the separateness of the agent and the beneficiary?

The Topic of Altruism in Moral Philosophy

Altruism is generally contrasted with egoism. Where egoism is understood to be devotion to one's own interests as an action-guiding principle, altruism is taken to be devotion to the interests of others. In this polarisation, the articulation of egoism in theory is usually taken to be unproblematic; the agent's devotion to his own interests is taken for granted. Altruism is the problem: why should anyone be concerned about the interests of others?[2] Furthermore, it is frequently assumed that self-interested acts cannot be intrinsically moral, and that only other-regarding acts that are motivated by others' interests qualify as moral. And then the issue becomes how one might persuade others to be moral since it seems that we cannot appeal to their own interests in trying to persuade them. This question is at the heart of much modern moral philosophy.

On the other hand, the dominant model of rationality in rational choice theory assumes that anyone who chooses to act is trying to achieve some purpose of his, and that his actions can be assessed as rational or not according to whether he is efficient and effective in his choice of means. This implies that the purposes pursued in rational action are the interests of those who act, and that the criterion of rationality is efficiency and effectiveness. This view is not confined to philosophical discussion: it has become a commonplace to expect selfish motives for any action. Anyone who goes to some trouble, who takes on himself the costs and burdens of some work, is presumed to seek some advantage to himself which outweighs the burdens involved; otherwise the action must appear to be irrational, a waste of effort. Familiar counter-examples as, for instance, parents who assume burdens for the benefit of their children are dismissed: the parents are presumed to seek the satisfaction of parenting.[3] By implication activity directed exclusively to the interests of others cannot count as rational.

A paradox emerges from these two elements: self-interested action cannot be moral, and other-directed action cannot be rational. Many philosophical discussions of altruism are directed to circumventing or dissolving this paradox. For instance, in the collection of essays referred to, one essay begins by asking whether acts of altruism can be rational,[4] while another attempts to show that self-interested acts could be moral.[5] A third attempts to locate reasons for action in some shared reality which transcends the dichotomy of self-interest and other-interest.[6]

In the other branches of philosophy in which altruism is now widely discussed, the polarisation with egoism is also particularly marked. Theoretical models of rationality built on the choices of a self-interested individual have dominated theory in the social sciences, especially economics and politics. Liberal political philosophy and liberal economics see society as the outcome of bargaining and contract between individual agents who pursue their own good. On this view, action which benefits others must be motivated by the benefit which the agent expects for himself. And therefore altruism is a problem. If there were pure instances of it, they would be unexplainable, and in turn, would be incapable of explaining social inter-action. One particular paradigm of rationality is operative here, namely, instrumental rationality based on the relation of means to goals. It is rational to choose effective means when one pursues a goal, and it is also rational to be efficient in the use of those means. This is indeed a valid sense of rationality, and the basis of useful criteria for evaluating action in a broad spectrum. However, it is not the only conceivable model of rationality. The limits of theory based on this model are becoming evident and several critics have documented the deficiencies of theory due to exclusive reliance on this model.[7] At the same time, they are looking for a broader understanding of practical rationality which would enable them to explain the complexity of forms of human cooperation and social ordering without having to rely exclusively on self-interest. Altruism is often the obvious candidate for an alternative to self-interest. As well as the theoretical concern, empirical studies are documenting forms of community which are not reducible to the interests of contracting individuals.[8] Here again the alternative to the rationality of the egoistic individual is frequently named altruism.

IS ALTRUISM THE KEY?

The analysis of action in terms of the interests of individuals is a powerful instrument in social philosophy. It is powerful in underlining the need for coordination and cooperation. But it belongs in the stable of a long line of powerful philosophical tools which allow one to find common ground in the context of competition and conflict. In the context of competing material interests, and mutually opposed religious convictions and philosophical world-views, negotiation and argument must find some agreed starting point. The strategy is to identify interests which one can presume the opponent must have, no matter how his opinions and ideals differ from one's own. So one can appeal to the other's interest in survival and security, or his interest in liberty to pursue his goals, or his interest in efficiency or competency, or his desire for as big a share as possible of the means which he will need to achieve whatever goals he may have.[9] In each case, the argument can proceed on a minimal basis, and when successful, conclude to quite an elaborate account of social order. This is why the model of individualist, instrumental rationality is so successful in economic and political science: it allows for the construction of elaborate theory on the basis of minimalist and seemingly incontrovertible assumptions.

This is the usefulness of the analysis: appeal to self-interest in a context of conflict in which the opponent's interests are jeopardised. It is a powerful and valuable tool. However, it may be misapplied in situations which are not so totally conflicted. The arguments which we conduct with one another do not always have to begin with a search for common ground and the construction of a starting point. Often we are already involved in common projects and shared activities. Indeed, social and economic life would not be possible at all were there not significant areas of common ground and shared interests. But how do we make sense of this communality and co-operation? And how might society foster and encourage its members to participate in public projects for reasons other than self-interest?

HOW TO COMBINE SELF-INTEREST AND OTHER-INTEREST?

If people are taught to assess rationality in terms of the interests of actors, they will always find it difficult to consider as rational action which is explained primarily in terms of the interests of others. At the same time the success of explanatory models using the notion of self-interest will encourage people to think in these terms. Is it not inevitable that a moral and legal system which builds on individual interests, perhaps modelled on property rights, will foster a culture in which people learn to be self-interested, are trained to think in terms of their own advantage, and accustom themselves to ridicule 'do-gooders' who speak of the common good or duties and obligations to others? Can the two elements of self-interest and altruism be combined at all, even in such a limited way as 'altruism in formulating the laws, and self-interest in acting within them'?[10] As Aristotle would put it, the law is the great educator which trains and disciplines subjects to know and act for the good. Where then are people to acquire the altruism needed for making law, when the law which has educated them has formed them to be people who regard their own interests? Once again it is Rousseau who provides a clear delineation of the problem. He sees a tragic tension between the interests of individuals and the public interest. Private reason contradicts public reason, and therefore the appeals by spiritual and political leaders for citizens to care for the well-being of all will be ineffectual. 'What is one to think of an interaction where the reason of each private individual dictates to him maxims directly contrary to those that public reason preaches to the body of society, and where each finds his profit in the misfortune of another?'[11]

Rather than contributing to social and cultural cohesion, pursuit of a solution in terms of altruism may lead to further disintegration of the social fabric. The danger is that institutions in society like the churches and educational bodies will be asked to train people in altruism, when the message communicated by the market, including competition for university places and jobs, is that self-interest is the only rational stance. Teachers and preachers would increasingly find themselves on the margins and outside the mainstream of the serious business of society.

The political rhetoric which is required not only to make sense of people's willingness to cooperate but also to offer persuasive arguments to encourage greater efforts in common ventures cannot be based on the disjunction egoism–altruism. These terms function in their appropriate contexts because they abstract from the content of the interests concerned, and identify those whose interests are at stake: does someone act for his own interests, or for the interests of others? Abstraction from the content of the interests made sense where one sought common ground in the context of conflict without presuming too much of one's opponent. However, cooperation, common ventures, whether on the small scale or on the large scale in politics and society, require shared convictions on the interests at stake. Many have remarked on how nationalism provided this perspective alongside the restrictive approach of liberal democracy. Whether it be the language of nationalism or of some other world-view, we need a language for talking about our common interests, and a way of evaluating them. A vocabulary for speaking of the good and of the good life is the appropriate alternative to the language of interest, whether of self or another. In the next chapter, I will look at one possible alternative and assess its usefulness for explaining cooperation in society.

CHAPTER 4

THE COMMON GOOD OF PRACTICES

I n the preceding chapter I discussed the adequacy of altruism as an alternative explanatory model to that of individual interest to explain cooperative action. I rejected it because it retained the suppositions of the disjunction of egoism and altruism and offered to explain action only in terms of interests attributable to individuals. I concluded the chapter with the remark that an alternative is needed which would allow explanation in terms of interests or values which are shared. One possible alternative is that discussed by Alasdair MacIntyre.[1] Up to now I have used the scenario borrowed from Rousseau of someone coming to the aid of another in need in order to highlight the unacceptable implications of defining rationality in terms of interests. MacIntyre focuses on a different scenario. He asks us to reflect on our experiences of cooperation in local, small-scale communities. He suggests many examples, including sports clubs, professional associations, local political groups, fishing crews and farming communities. He invites us to focus on the way in which members cooperate because of a shared interest in the goods to be achieved through some activity. He distinguishes between forms of cooperation in which people share a delight in the achievement of excellence in their relevant activity, and other forms in which the dominant interest is the achievement of wealth, power, prestige or reputation. The two types of groups might well be engaged in the same kind of activity, but the goods which they strive for in that activity are very different.

In clarification of this point, he responded to the misunder-standing of critics by elaborating the contrast between two kinds of fishing crews, sketching ideal types.[2] In one crew, the owner of the boat might be oriented to maximising her profits, while the crew members are concerned primarily about the size of their earnings. In such a situation, individuals will pull out or the owner will redirect her investment, as earnings fall below a critical minimum. By contrast, another crew could exhibit devotion to excellence in fishing and to excellence in playing one's part as member of such a crew. This would extend beyond the actual activities involved in the fishing itself.

> The dependence of each member on the qualities of character and skills of others will be accompanied by a recognition that from time to time one's own life will be in danger and that whether one drowns or not may depend upon someone else's courage. And the consequent concern of each member of the crew for the others, if it is to have the stamp of genuine concern, will characteristically have to extend to those for whom those others care: the members of their immediate families.[3]

He remarks further how for members of such a crew con-tinuing allegiance to one's fellows and one's community will not depend on economic rewards alone.

The contrast between these two types of fishing crews cor-responds to a distinction between two kinds of goods, which MacIntyre labels external and internal. Earnings from fishing are an example of an external good. Such goods tend to be extrinsic to the activities through which they are pursued; if more money can be made through fish-farming rather than fishing, then the efforts will be redirected. External goods are also such that they can be distributed so that one having more means another having less. The more that is taken by the boat owner as profit, the less there is left for the crew. By contrast internal goods are intrinsic to the activities in which they are pursued, and the achievement of them benefits all equally. In the case of the fishing crew, the internal goods are the achieve-ment of excellence in the exercise of the craft of fishing, and the living of a kind of life built around this activity. A fishing community which honours its best fishermen is not necessarily acknowledging those who have earned the most. Further, the achievement of excellence by some, which might merit honour from their peers, is to the benefit of all who share the interest in such excellence. This point might be clearer from the example of the pursuit of chess, which MacIntyre frequently uses. Creativity and ingenuity in the game, and the creation of a new strategy, set a new standard for chess players in general and thereby benefit all who are involved. MacIntyre stresses that internal goods may only be had from participation in the relevant activity, and that they cannot be known apart from such participation.

PRACTICES

Forms of cooperation in pursuit of internal goods are called practices. By this term MacIntyre means

> . . . any coherent and complex form of socially established cooperative human activity through which goods internal to that form of activity are realised in the course of trying to achieve those standards of excellence which are appropriate to, and partially definitive of that form of activity, with the result that human powers to achieve excellence, and human conceptions of the ends and goods involved, are systematically extended.[4]

The healing and teaching professions can provide examples of practices in this sense. An individual teacher measures herself against standards of excellence set by the best teachers she has encountered herself. In her work she strives to accomplish the goods which are internal to the teaching activity, namely, the development of the student and his acquisition of skills and competencies and mastery of a curriculum. Success in this project includes the achievement for the teacher herself of a good intrinsic to the quality of her own life. To give a significant part of one's life to the work of teaching is to make the quality of one's life as a whole dependent partially at least on the quality of one's teaching. A life devoted to the pursuit of excellence which exhibits some measure of achievement is

experienced as worthwhile, and so there is the additional
good of a flourishing life as a teacher internal to the practice
of teaching. Furthermore, MacIntyre's notion of practice
includes the openness to development such that the achievement of excellence in the pursuit of internal goods can lead
to the revision and expansion of the understanding of what is
involved in the teaching relationship. The individual teacher
does strive to achieve standards which had been set by others,
but her own performance and achievement can in turn lead
to a redefinition of what constitutes good teaching.

What sorts of qualities would teachers have to possess in
order to be able to succeed in a life devoted to the pursuit of
excellence? In answering this question MacIntyre discusses the
notion of virtue. He understands virtue as qualities which tend
to enable their possessors to achieve the goods internal to
practices. Examples are fairness, honesty, truthfulness and
temperance in the sense of self-control. But while his main
interest is in the understanding of virtue, MacIntyre's discussion provides us with the possibility of a new approach to the
notion of the common good. Practices are forms of cooperation which are to be understood in terms of internal goods.
So teaching is a form of cooperative activity to be understood
in terms of the internal goods of human development and
the acquisition of skills and knowledge. These goods are valued
by all who cooperate, and are therefore common goods within
the practice of teaching. A shared understanding and valuing
of those goods is what provides the bond of unity in a teaching–
learning community, and enables a cadre of teachers to understand themselves as cooperating in a joint project. Among the
internal goods which they will share is some grasp of what it
means to have lived a good life as a teacher. And so the stories
of individual teachers' lives are embedded in the broader
stories of the practice of teaching and of the tradition of education. The story of a life is an account of successes and failures
in striving for those goods for the sake of which one cooperates
with others.

I am suggesting therefore that MacIntyre's discussion of
practices provides a possible scenario for understanding

cooperation in terms other than that of self-interest. Those who give of themselves in a joint effort do so for the sake of internal goods which they value along with others. Unlike external goods such as money which can be divided up and distributed so that one getting more means another getting less, internal goods benefit all who cooperate in a practice and cannot be divided up. A student's mastery of a musical instrument benefits all, as is clear from the shared delight in a wonderful performance. Since the achievement of the internal goods of a practice benefits all involved, the question of 'whose good?' does not arise. Accordingly, the issue typical of the disjunction egoism–altruism, namely, does the agent pursue her own interests or those of others, is inappropriate. The goods pursued are the goods of a community, shared in their pursuit and in their enjoyment.

Of course, such situations are precarious and vulnerable, as MacIntyre admits. The possibility of corruption for the sake of external goods is always present. We can imagine for instance a local choir, perhaps attached to a church community, whose members enjoy music and singing and the friendship with one another which has grown out of this common activity and shared interest. The quality of their interaction can be undermined by the emergence of a particularly gifted singer who insists on being treated as the *prima donna* she considers herself to be, or by the appointment of a new organist in the church who is jealous of his official position and power and who insists on taking control. If such personalities cannot enter into the practice and subordinate their own wishes to the values shared by the group, their agenda will dominate, and others will be increasingly reluctant to participate in activity in which the issues of power and prestige and fame are to the fore. Some will drop out of the choir, not because there is no more singing, but because they can no longer realise the internal goods in the activity which all members formerly jointly valued.

This example can also serve to elucidate MacIntyre's definition of virtue in relation to practices. Virtues, he suggests, are acquired human qualities, the possession of which tends to facilitate one's achievement of the goods internal to practices.

So for instance, the lack of fairness in acknowledging and rewarding the contributions of all the members to the choir, which is associated with the star's monopolising of the limelight, is detrimental to the achievement of the good of the choir and the survival of the practice. Also, the lack of temperance, reflected in the star singer's inability to distance herself from her personal need for admiration and to relativise it to the goods of the group, is the reason why the group disintegrates. Perhaps also the lack of courage on the part of members who realise what is going on, but are unwilling to speak up and confront those whose self-interestedness is threatening the joint activity, also contributes to the ending of the practice. For courage is the willingness to accept risks to oneself for the sake of the goods of the community.

Virtues are important for the survival of practices and for the achievement of their internal goods. In his further discussion of institutions in relation to practices MacIntyre again emphasises the need for virtues to limit what he calls the corrupting power of institutions. Practices are distinguished from institutions, as the practice of chess is to be distinguished from the chess club, and the practice of teaching is to be distinguished from the school or university. Yet, MacIntyre asserts, no practice can survive for any length of time without the support of institutions. Institutions therefore are accredited with a very positive role in relation to the sustaining of practices. Little further is said about this positive role, except that the activity of creating and maintaining institutions has itself all the characteristics of a practice.[5] The positive role of institutions is only mentioned in passing, but their negative aspect in the threat they pose to practices is emphasised. As internal goods are achieved in practices, institutions deal in external goods. Institutions allocate power and distribute rewards such as income, social status and reputation. Competition to acquire these external goods, which of their nature cannot be shared, can so predominate human interaction that the spirit of cooperation in pursuit of shared internal goods is deadened. Then the practice is swamped by the institution which should have sustained it. The choir from the example above can only attract those who are interested in achieving a public profile, social status or a platform from which to exercise influence. The medical and educational institutions which are needed to sustain the practices of healing and teaching can threaten those practices when conflict over status, remuneration and access to resources shifts the focus of attention away from the internal goods of healing and teaching. MacIntyre considers that the virtues such as justice, courage and truthfulness are the only safeguard against the tendency of institutions to corrupt practices.

EXPLANATION IN TERMS OF PRACTICES

The usefulness of MacIntyre's ideas for my topic should be evident from this summary presentation. He provides one possibility of understanding forms of cooperation in terms of goods which are common. While this is in contrast to explanatory models which are predicated on the interests of individuals, it also allows an incorporation of those other models. By means of his parallel distinctions of internal and external goods on the one hand, and practices and institutions on the other, he can explain how cooperative activity in pursuit of internal goods may deteriorate into competitive activity for external goods. His discussion also makes clear that an exclusive reliance on the notion of the self-interest of actors would prevent one from grasping the distinctive nature of practices and cooperation in pursuit of internal goods. Indeed he goes even further to suggest that 'without the virtues there could be a recognition only of what I have called external goods and not at all of internal goods in the context of practices. And in any society which recognised only external goods competitiveness would be the dominant and even exclusive feature'.[6]

Explanation of cooperation beyond the ambit of self-interest, as suggested by MacIntyre, is in terms of internal goods. Such goods are many and complex. He distinguishes three distinct kinds of good, 'those internal to practices, those which are the goods of an individual life, and those which are the goods of community'.[7] Both for individual lives and for communities, an ongoing issue is the ordering of goods, allocating priorities, as for instance between the goods of chess, of parenting and of fishing. Within small-scale communities based on practices there is a shared view of the good life which provides an ordering principle for subordinate goods.[8]

THE COMMON GOOD AGAINST THE NATION STATE

I am looking for a way of explaining cooperation. What is needed is a theory or explanatory scheme which can enable us to make sense of cooperation without having to reduce it to the pursuit by individuals of their own interests. It should be clear from the second chapter that there are major limitations attached to the self-interest model. MacIntyre's discussion of practices and the internal goods which are the common goods of those cooperating in them provides a possible solution. It allows us to identify reasons for action which are shared and irreducible to interests. It therefore seems promising for my purposes. The difficulty is, however, that MacIntyre explicitly denies the applicability of these ideas of internal goods, practices and communities to the politics of the modern state. He expressly contrasts the kind of cooperation based on practices found in small-scale local community, and the kind of cooperation characteristic of the modern state. Linked to this contrast are juxtaposed views on the human person and on the nature of the good. In what follows, I will present his argument and then investigate if he is correct in excluding talk of the common good from modern politics.

MacIntyre is not the only contemporary author with an interest in the common good. Amitai Etzioni, Michael J. Sandel and Robert N. Bellah are frequently referred to as communitarians because of their advocacy of a base for politics in community rather than in the interests of individuals.[9] Although he is frequently linked to this group, MacIntyre disassociates himself from their position on two points. First of all, he maintains that he does not advocate anything or promote any particular cause, unlike the communitarians who do take an advocacy stance. MacIntyre maintains that he merely describes what goes on, and while his description may be mistaken, he is not saying what people ought to be doing or ought to be thinking. The second point on which he distances himself from communitarians is in regard to the modern nation state. He understands the communitarians to be advocating a particular style of politics in the nation state. Communitarians would want the nation state to embody community to some degree, as if politics should arise out of a shared view of the good. MacIntyre, by contrast, has little hope for the nation state and would resist strongly any attempt to have its politics rooted in a conception of community. And so he is adamant that he is not engaged in an attempt to reform the modern state.[10]

In distancing himself from the reforming aspirations of the communitarians, MacIntyre has revealed the extent of his disregard for the modern state and its politics. He thinks that the contemporary state cannot be reformed in the way advocated by communitarians, and he agrees with liberals that modern nation states which masquerade as embodiments of community are always to be resisted. This stance, of course, is not based on any particular regard for the modern state: on the contrary, the modern nation state is, in his view,

> . . . a dangerous and unmanageable institution, presenting itself on the one hand as a bureaucratic supplier of goods and services, which is always about to, but never actually does, give its clients value for money, and on the other hand as a repository of sacred values, which from time to time invites one to lay down one's life on its behalf. As I have remarked elsewhere, it is like being asked to die for the telephone company.[11]

MacIntyre draws a sharp contrast between the common good and the public interest. The common good he describes as the good of a type of association not reducible to the goods of individual members, but in turn partly constitutive of their good. Not every human association has a common good in the sense intended. Such association would of necessity have to be local and self-regulating, so that members could not attain their good without participating in the association's self-regulation. This involves continual debate and disagreement, but such dialogue is conducted with a high degree of public visibility within the association. By contrast, the good of the modern state is typically said to be the public interest. As a good, it is not constitutive of the goods of individual members; the state is seen as external to individual members as a means to their interests. Every citizen benefits to some degree from the achievements of the state, but usually there is disagreement about how contributions and costs and benefits are to be distributed. The typical problem is that of the free-rider, since it is always in the individual's interest to benefit without having to bear a share of the costs. Unlike the transparent discourse of local community, MacIntyre maintains, conflicts in modern states are typically resolved by bargains done behind closed doors which are then made public in some socially acceptable guise. Having contrasted the politics of the common good and the politics of the public interest, MacIntyre maintains that the two are mutually antagonistic. The state always requires the systematic subordination of local community to itself and its agencies; and the skills required for successful participation in national politics are detrimental to the virtues required for participation in local community.

The Contemporary Moral Vacuum

This polarisation between the two types of association and their respective goods comes from MacIntyre's discussion of the history of ethics in *After Virtue*. That book is an argument about the lack of a shared language for conducting moral debate today. There is no agreement on ultimate principles for the resolution of contemporary disputes such as those about the permissibility of abortion, the use of military force or the distribution of property. His study of the history of ethics is intended to show how the moral vacuum at the heart of modern society had come about. He documents the disintegration of a shared moral vocabulary such that there are no principles and values on which agreement can be sustained which allow modern societies to handle their conflict. Of course this dilemma for moral discourse has implications for politics. Government in the modern state cannot express or represent a moral community of citizens. Instead, according to MacIntyre, government is simply a set of institutional arrangements for imposing a bureaucratised unity on a society that lacks genuine moral consensus. According to the ideas of political theorists like Hobbes, Locke, Hume or Mill, contemporary society is made up of 'a collection of citizens of nowhere who have banded together for their common protection'.[12] They do not share a conception of the community's good as specified by the good for humans in general,[13] but see society as 'an arena in which individuals seek to secure what is useful or agreeable to them'.[14] Accordingly, 'conflict and not consensus is at the heart of modern social structure' and modern politics is neither based on nor creative of genuine moral consensus.[15] Rather, modern politics is civil war carried on by other means. Government and law, if it is unable to represent a moral consensus of society, must appear to citizens as a set of institutional arrangements for imposing a bureaucratised unity on society, and so can hardly evoke their allegiance and loyalty.[16] In the resulting moral vacuum the nature of political obligation becomes systematically unclear. Why anyone would obey the law, obey the government which happens to rule, cannot be explained in terms of a virtue of patriotism or of loyalty to country. The contrast between the liberal state and the kind of small-scale community which sustains practices is drawn by means of these remarks. Unlike the shared valuing of internal goods which unites members of communities sustaining practices, there is no consensus on values uniting the citizen body of a modern state.[17] Accordingly, the modern state cannot have a common good which is a genuine good, other than the public interest.

MacIntyre has emphasised that he is not attempting to reform the modern state, but merely to describe its nature. He admits that there are many tasks to be performed by government in modern states. The rule of law has to be vindicated, injustice and unwarranted suffering have to be dealt with, liberty has to be defended in ways that are sometimes only possible through the use of governmental institutions. The whole analysis involves a polarising contrast between, on the one hand, the tradition of the virtues which has its best expression, perhaps, in Aristotle, and, on the other hand, the modern nation state which is rooted in a moral vacuum. This juxtaposition, as MacIntyre has drawn it, sees a place for the concept of the common good only in the description of the type of community in which the virtues can be practised. By contrast, there is no role for a concept of common good in the description of the contemporary nation state. If MacIntyre is correct in this view, then his notion of practices is not as useful for my purposes as it seemed at first glance. There is no great advantage in having an explanatory model for cooperation which is confined to local small-scale community, and which has no application in the larger social and political scale. And so it must be asked whether MacIntyre is correct in his pessimistic view of the liberal state and its politics. I want to propose that there is a meaningful sense in which the modern state can be said to have a common good. Accordingly, I take issue with MacIntyre on this point. Where did he go wrong?

WHERE MACINTYRE WENT WRONG

I want to suggest that MacIntyre makes a mistake in regard to the relation between the state and the common good, and that this mistake stems from his particular understanding of types of goods. His discussion of internal and external goods is an essential element of his creative contribution in *After Virtue* to the reconstruction of an Aristotelian concept of virtue. But a distortion arises, I will argue, because elements constructed to serve one purpose are made to serve another for which they were not originally intended.

INSTITUTIONS AS GOODS

My suggestion is that when MacIntyre considers the common good, his thought spontaneously slips into the dichotomy between internal and external goods. The question of the common good seems to become the question whether the common good comprises external or internal goods. Recall his distinctions between internal and external goods, and between practices and institutions. Teaching is a practice, and a school is an institution; students' development is an internal good, and a tenured position is an external good. External goods are not capable of being shared: they are typically what people compete for, and so, it would seem, the notion of common good, with the emphasis on what is common, must be confined to internal goods. This is plausible of course, since internal goods were introduced precisely as that for the sake of which people cooperate in coherent and complex forms of socially established activity. It seems then that common goods will only be found in forms of association which are practices; institutions, and that includes states, will be dealing in external goods, and so, it would seem, cannot have a common good.

This is a trap. The distinction between internal and external in regard to the goods pursued in activities does not exhaust the range of human good. What about institutions themselves? What kind of good are they? It is clear that MacIntyre considers institutions to have a positive role relative to practices, although they are also a source of threat. Institutions are essential for the survival of practices and he even suggests that the activity of creating and maintaining institutions might constitute a practice.[18] So what kind of good are they? It seems that they cannot simply be identified with either internal or external goods. Take for instance a college chess club. It is a good for the students and for the college. It sustains the practice of chess, the internal goods of which are closely linked to those of academic practices. Certainly it may deal in external goods like prizes and reputation and official roles which will look good on a student's CV. But the club itself is not an external good in that sense. Neither is it an internal good. This pair of terms is not useful in considering the kind of good the chess club is: another range of categories is needed.

I suggest that the key is to be found in the relationship between activities as means and their corresponding ends. MacIntyre has suggested that the activities of practices are means to internal goods, but they are such that they are intrinsic to those goods. The good of excellence in performance is not separable from the performance. By contrast the means to external goods are separable from the goods: money can be made by fishing or fish-farming. Institutions sustain practices and facilitate the achievement of their internal goods while at the same time enabling the pursuit of external goods. The goodness of institutions resides in this dual role. The corresponding activities however are extrinsic to both the internal goods and the external. Writing the minutes of the chess club committee meeting is some distance from the practice of chess itself; *a fortiori*, attending a meeting of a college finance committee responsible for allocating funds to student activities is far removed from the internal goods of chess. Yet such institutional activities are intended to and frequently do in fact contribute to sustaining the practice with its internal goods.

This thought could be elaborated further, and one could attempt to trace the interconnections between different layers of organisations and different types of institutions. The philosophy department, the college, the university, the Higher Education Authority, the Department of Education, all impinge in some way on the quantity and quality of the individual student's experience of the learning–teaching relationship in the discipline of philosophy. The contribution which each organisation makes to that experience can be assessed in relation to the practices concerned. To the extent that they sustain the practices with their internal goods, they would seem to be good. The relevant internal goods are achieved in greater or lesser degree: knowledge of the history of philosophical debate is fostered, the skills of critical thinking are developed, and the quality of public discourse is enriched. The institutions concerned are seen to contribute to sustaining practices with their internal goods, and as such, they would belong to the common good of those who participate in the practices. Furthermore, all those who do not themselves participate in the relevant practices, but wish it to be the case that many such practices flourish, would have to value as part of their common good the institutions which sustain the practices. Therefore the common good of people cooperating in practices is not necessarily confined to internal goods, but includes the institutional means which sustain the practices. Needless to say, MacIntyre's warnings about the corrupting power of institutions are relevant. Without the virtues, those who operate the institutions can soon become the enemy of practices. To be virtuous however would require that they value what they do beyond the pay-off to themselves, and for that they would need a language which enables them to express the rationality of their collaboration in terms beyond the interests of individuals.

THE GOOD LIFE REQUIRES A RANGE OF GOODS

I have been arguing that MacIntyre is misled by his distinction between internal and external goods to think that only internal goods can be common goods in a proper sense, and that he is not able to consider the manner in which institutions can be valued as common goods. That he is so misled is surprising when one considers Aristotle's own treatment of the question. After all, MacIntyre is trying to rescue an Aristotelian understanding of moral language, and specifically virtue. But Aristotle was not trapped by a distinction between internal and external goods; he recognised the need for a wide range of goods if one is to achieve the good life. This is very noticeable in his discussion of the requirements for the ideal city and of the essential conditions of *eudaemonia*, usually translated as happiness, well-being, or human flourishing.[19] His virtuous citizen required access to a range of goods including material resources. And in his discussion of friendship, his category was broad enough to include relationships based on usefulness and on pleasure. The benefits of access to status and social prestige are among the goods which Aristotle recognises people pursue in their friendships. His categories of good and of friendship do not require him to exclude these, simply because they are in MacIntyre's terms external goods. Unlike Aristotle, MacIntyre does not consider a range of goods, but focuses rather on the polarity of internal and external goods. While this distinction is useful to him in reconstructing the concept of virtue, it introduces a distortion when applied in the context of the common good. It is helpful in overcoming a tendency to see everything in terms of interests, and so enables us to envisage cooperation for the sake of goods which are not assignable to particular people as their exclusive interests. But MacIntyre seems to suggest that the common good is confined to internal goods. That external goods could not be common makes sense if the concept of external good is introduced exclusively with examples like power and wealth; these usually are seen to be distributed rather than shared. But how are we to understand the goods pursued by states and institutions: for example, security, social stability, welfare, level of crime, level of literacy, employment rates, stability of currency, in other words, the typical indicators which are relied upon for policy making, which are not simply external, but definitely not internal either? Aristotle could consider these as common goods, whereas MacIntyre seems unable to.

WHAT DOES MACINTYRE OPPOSE?

In the discussion above I have reported many of MacIntyre's critical remarks concerning the liberal state and its politics. To the extent that it is inhospitable to the cultivation of the virtues and the pursuit of internal goods in practices, MacIntyre sees the politics of the liberal state in negative terms. There is a tone of nostalgia in his criticisms: he seems to long for another age in which politics would once again be rooted in a moral consensus. And yet he refuses to join the communitarian appeal for a return to community. What then is his point? Is the liberal state without any redeeming features in his opinion, or is it that he sees no possibility of improving it? Here again I would suggest that MacIntyre is misled by his own positive contribution to draw conclusions which are inappropriate. He is correct in pointing out that whereas the political community of Athens provided the social milieu for the life of the virtues as Aristotle understood them, the modern state is not the appropriate social context for virtues and practices as MacIntyre has defined them; these have their place rather in local small-scale community. However, this fact alone would not explain the strength of his antipathy to the liberal state. That seems to be due to the way in which the modern state is linked to the idea of self-interest. Those in the tradition of Hobbes and Locke, Hume and Mill who explain the rationale of the state rely on self-interest in some form as the key to understanding individuals' motivation to cooperate with others. As well as being defended by a theoretical articulation of a rationality of self-interest, the modern state also fosters self-interested activity. MacIntyre points to 'its individualism, its acquisitiveness, and its elevation of the values of the market to a central social place'.[20] The self-understanding of the liberal state amounts to an explicit rejection of an Aristotelian perspective on the goods of cooperation and on the virtues. This opposition between Aristotelian and liberal is at the heart of his critique of the modern state. In what follows and in the following chapters, I will take issue with MacIntyre on this point. I will attempt to show that there is the possibility of an accommodation between an Aristotelian conception of the goods of cooperation and a liberal position on the nature and function of the state.

POLITICS AND CONFLICT

MacIntyre is very pessimistic about modern politics and the contemporary nation state. His reasons for this have to do with the inherent inhospitality of modern politics towards virtue and the virtuous life. But while he has written a history of the concept of virtue, and discussed the problems of writing such a history, he has not written a history of the concept of politics or even of the virtues attached to ruling or government. If we were to attempt to write a similar history of the concept of politics as he has done in regard to virtue, I think we could preserve a role for the concept of common good in describing the activities of the modern state.

The polarity which MacIntyre has drawn between community in the Aristotelian sense in which virtues can be exercised, and the modern nation state, relies very much on a contrast between consensus and conflict. The community in which virtues can be exercised is presumed to be based upon a shared view of the good, on consensus in regard to the meaning and purpose of life. As a result there would also be public consensus in regard to the excellences and activities which would be valued and praised and those which would be discouraged.[21] For Aristotle, and perhaps it could be said for the classical world in general, the point of politics and of political community is a moral one. It is to achieve the good life, which involves the formation of citizens in virtue, so that they will live noble lives, distinguished by acts of justice and virtue.[22] The modern political community, by contrast, is premised on conflict, on the expectation that there is no common good, no shared view of the good life. The tradition of modern political thought from Hobbes to the present day assumes that there is conflict, and that the task is to find ways of handling conflict without resort to force. While that contrast between the Aristotelian and the modern as presented here seems to be one between polar opposites, the historical development from the expectation of consensus to the assumption of conflict has not been so sudden. If this history were to be written I think it would allow us to conclude that MacIntyre's polarisation, while helpful in his discussion of moral language, is not so faithful to the analysis of politics.

In contrasting practice-based communities and the modern liberal state, MacIntyre remarked that the state is not qualified to perform the role of moral educator as were Aristotelian-style communities. The unsuitability of the state as moral educator was first remarked by Augustine in his *The City of God*. This fifth-century document can be taken as representing the abandonment of the classical expectation of moral consensus as found in Plato and Aristotle. Unlike the Greek philosophers who hoped for harmony and unity, Augustine expects the political arena to be conflictual. He explains this in terms of the radical tension throughout all of human affairs between the 'City of God' and the 'earthly city'.[23] The radical disorder brought about by the rebellious assertion of human will means that human action and human structures are largely motivated by the *libido dominandi,* the desire to dominate others, and by the pride whereby one seeks to make a name for oneself and achieve a place in posterity by successful participation in the affairs of one's city. As a result, the status of the political community was relativised. It was no longer to be seen as the forum in which the common good or the supreme good would be pursued and achieved; only in the context of the City of God, in Augustine's sense, could the highest good for the human and the human's common good be realised. The most that political institutions could hope to achieve is an inferior good, which Augustine refers to as 'temporal peace and justice'. But while this good of security and civil peace might be seen as an inferior good, it was nonetheless a genuine good and a common good for all those who would participate in maintaining and indeed benefiting from political community.

Augustine expressly addressed the question of the good or virtuous person as to whether or not he should withdraw from political life and participation in those institutions which serve public order and security. The question would arise precisely because of the inevitable involvement of such people in institutions which did not only good but sometimes harm. He considered particularly the position of judge, which seemed to be linked inevitably to injustice and miscarriages of justice. Augustine was adamant that it would be wrong for the virtuous person to withdraw completely from political life and that such a person had a duty, for the sake of human well-being, to contribute as best he could in the office of judge or ruler.[24] Augustine, for one, therefore, would not be happy with MacIntyre's relegation of the pursuit of the good and of the common good to small local familiar community, whether it be at the level of family or neighbourhood or interest group, or indeed church.

Perhaps MacIntyre would have no difficulty with Augustine's rather negative position on the state and its scope for action. However, he may not be allowed to rest there. The evolution of structures of government in western states through a complex history has been accompanied by a rich body of philosophical reflection. That reflection has raised questions which may not be dismissed. The starting point of much of Enlightenment and post-Enlightenment political philosophy has been the recognition of the fact that there is no shared view of the human good and there is no social consensus on the principles to regulate conflict. At the same time, the sources of conflict in human psychology, in diversity of interests and desires, in the multiplicity of ideologies and world-views and in the indeterminacy of some disputes, have been increasingly recognised. The philosophies which took this as their starting point have looked for some way of coordinating social life and establishing some order in the midst of threatening disorder. Even if one were to concede to MacIntyre that the Enlightenment project of establishing that order on the basis of some understanding of a neutral rationality has failed, the starting problem remains the problem which political philosophy today must also address.

<h2 style="text-align:center">The Good of Public Order</h2>

It is to be noted that the failure which MacIntyre alleges is a failure to provide a coherent moral justification. But the distinction which is suggested by Augustine's thought and explicitly developed more recently, between the common good in an unrestricted sense and a more restricted public order as the ambit of state action, might allow us to accept that the desired coherent moral justification could only be hoped for within the horizon of the unrestricted common good, which is not achievable with the instruments available to participants in conflicted social reality. Only agreement on what can help establish and maintain public order can realistically be aimed at in political action and debate.[25] It is this distinction which would have to be reconstructed and incorporated in the writing of a history of the concept of politics. As noted, the distinction between a fundamental moral justification and a political justification is paralleled by a distinction between the unrestricted horizon of the good, in which the common good in the full sense would have its place, and a restricted horizon of public order. MacIntyre has drawn attention to a particular difficulty in writing such a history, namely, that the historian herself would have to be able to adopt the mind-set in which the distinction and its elements have their place, and such an achievement has its conditions, which are not easily realised.[26] My argument, directed to some extent against MacIntyre, is that the institutions and procedures created from the concern for public order in the midst of threatening disorder, as well as the bodies of ideas which support those institutions and procedures and enable them to be changed and improved, both are genuine goods, and are common goods for those who cooperate in designing, operating and improving them. For MacIntyre to accept this argument, he would have to make two adjustments. He would have to expand his classification of goods, and he would have to recognise that the category of common good is not restricted to what he has called internal goods. I raised the first of these questions above in asking what kind of good a chess club is, since it is neither an internal nor an external good in MacIntyre's sense. The second question I raise now in considering the practical rationality of those who cooperate in maintaining public institutions.

When we consider the activities of those who, over generations, have worked to improve the quality of our law making and the quality of our legal institutions, who have worked to eliminate difficulties and problems and to improve formulations and processes, then it is difficult to see how we could make sense of this without reference to a genuine concern – at least on the part of some – for these structures and the services they provide. As elements in the practical rationality of people cooperating, these structures and services function as common goods. Of course, this is not to deny what MacIntyre points to, namely, the existence of people and groups who pursue a narrowly conceived self-interest in public institutions. We can acknowledge that there are those whose concern is limited to external goods such as money, influence and power. But it is inconceivable that the institutions of our health system, our justice system and our educational system could have been produced without some people whose motivation was other than simply the pursuit of external goods. The care for the education of the citizen body, the care for their training in the language and skills of public debate, the care for the perfection of instruments of legal protection and redress, reflect a common good, shared by some at least of those who create, maintain and improve the relevant social institutions.[27] This is not a concern for the moral goodness of citizens or that they adopt a particular moral outlook, but it is nonetheless a common good to which reference would have to be made in explaining the relevant activity. Debates within political philosophy between different types of liberals, between liberals and civic republicans, between these and communitarians all certainly reflect conflict, but conflict within the context of commitment to achieving the goals which are appropriate to the modern state, namely that our conflict be handled in such a way that there is no resort to violence and that allows at the same time for the protection of the liberties and the rights of individuals. In Augustine's sense, that is indeed a good and a common good in the proper sense, even though it is not the complete and supreme good or the highest common good in Aristotle's sense.

ADAPTING ARISTOTLE

Earlier in this chapter I suggested that this book is an attempt to reconcile elements of Aristotle's philosophy with central elements of liberalism. MacIntyre's polarisation of these two broad traditions suggests that the task is an impossible one. And so I have had to take issue with MacIntyre. In my argument I have resisted his tendency to confine the common good to the sphere of local community. I have argued that MacIntyre comes to this conclusion because of a particular distinction of goods useful to his purpose of writing a history of virtue. I have suggested that a discussion of politics and the common good in their own right would require a similar historical investigation, and I have argued that such an investigation could provide us with understandings of politics and the common good which would allow us to recognise a genuine common good in the politics of the modern state. In conclusion, it remains for me to show that my suggestion is a possible reconstruction of an Aristotelian position. Just as MacIntyre's own reconstruction of virtue is faithful to Aristotle only in some respects, abandoning some elements as conditioned by the particular social context of the Greek *polis*, so my defence could only aim at pointing to the Aristotelian inspiration of the ideas without claiming to recover the whole of his position.

There are three elements in my suggestion. First of all, I rely on a distinction between an unrestricted sense of common good and a restricted domain of public order. Secondly, I suggest that the politics of the modern state is concerned with the more restricted category. And thirdly, I maintain that public order is a genuine common good. This is faithful to Aristotle in some respects, and not in others. The proposition that public order is a genuine common good is consistent with the opening sentences of the *Politics*, Book I, chapter 1, in which Aristotle affirms that all associations aim at some good. The implication of this is that those who cooperate in the association have a common good which is expressed in the aim of their association. So my proposition that public order as the purpose of the modern state identifies a common good of politicians, administrators and citizens is an intelligibly Aristotelian position. Can the same be said for my distinction between unrestricted and restricted common goods? Aristotle recognises from the multiplicity of associations that there is a range of common goods, but also that there is a supreme good which embraces all the rest, and in the light of which all the rest can be ordered. The bones of my distinction therefore will not be strange to Aristotle. The major difference however is in the second proposition, in which the common good of politics is confined to the more restricted category. This marks a considerable break with Aristotle, for whom the *polis*, the political community, is the association which aims at the supreme good, that is, the good in relation to which all other goods are ordered. MacIntyre admits that the modern state cannot have this common good, but it is a mistake on his part to argue that it cannot have any common good.

In Book III of the *Politics* Aristotle expressly compares different views of the state and notes the limitations of the restricted views in comparison with his own. He identifies arrangements which are based on non-aggression pacts or assurances of mutual defence. He further identifies arrangements based on property ownership which are something like a business investment, and other arrangements based on agreements to exchange goods and services; these latter express the oligarch's view of the state.[28] On Aristotle's view, these forms of human cooperation, like all other communities, have a common good, whether it be security or economic well-being. But the goods they pursue are restricted in comparison with the good pursued by the best *polis*, namely the virtue and goodness of the citizens. 'So we must lay it down that the political association which we call a state exists not simply for the purpose of living together but for the sake of noble actions.' This state will also be concerned with security and economic well-being, but as subordinated to the complete well-being of the citizens, including their moral well-being. I agree with MacIntyre that the modern state cannot fulfil this role of making its citizens good in an unqualified sense. But the modern state, considered as one of the restricted political organisations described by Aristotle, does have its own common good, which is a genuine good. The question remains open whether that good is adequately characterised by phrases like security and economic well-being. The point at issue here is simply that the good which is the object of the modern state is a restricted good in comparison with the supreme good which Aristotle identified as the object of his best *polis*.

Finally, we might ask if the supreme good which Aristotle saw as the good of the *polis* could have any representation in the modern context. It seems evident that it could not be included as part of the overlapping consensus which sustains political institutions. But as a heuristic notion, it could make sense of the ongoing debate about politics and the good, and indeed of virtue. That history can be seen as an ongoing conversation, in the process of which problems are identified and solutions sought, questions are raised and answers are attempted, obstacles are encountered and overcome, partially or totally or not at all. This process of searching and questioning can be regarded as the generalised activity of politics in the sense in which Aristotle speaks of it in chapter 2 of Book I of the *Politics*, namely, as the participation in the discussion of what is useful and what is harmful, what is right and what is wrong, what is just and what is unjust. I will return to a consideration of this topic in a later chapter. But granted at this point that there is such an ongoing conversation, reflected for example in the development of the language of rights, and the specification of rights to be protected by law, then the dynamic of the debate points towards a resolution. The supreme common good can be understood as this ultimate resolution, which is shadowly intended in the orientation of these discussions; however, because there are always further questions, we know not to allow any particular instance of social order to claim to represent this supreme common good. In this sense therefore, it is arguable that my move away from Aristotle remains Aristotelian. And further, it is arguable that my move away from MacIntyre on the point of the common good remains consistent with what he writes elsewhere about the ongoing conversations which constitute traditions.

Conclusion

In this chapter I have explored MacIntyre's ideas on the good with a view to finding a theoretical explanation of cooperation beyond what is available on the model of self-interest. His analysis of practices draws our attention to the experience of taking part with others in collective pursuits. In joint activity we share goods internal to that activity, and jointly value lives built around such activity. And so MacIntyre does provide us with a way of understanding the common goods of cooperation. However, it might seem that this strategy is not viable for my purposes since MacIntyre explicitly excludes common goods from the politics of the modern state. I have queried this stance, drawing attention to his ambiguous attitude to institutions, his objection to the self-understanding of liberal politics while valuing some of its achievements, and the need for the recognition of a spectrum of goods beyond the polarisation of internal and external goods. Institutions can be good, and are recognised by MacIntyre as such, but they cannot be accommodated in his categorisation of goods into internal and external. Other concepts are needed. Valued for the functions they serve, institutions can be an element of the common good, and so there can be a common good appropriate to contemporary politics. The question then is whether there is a way of reconceiving the contemporary practice of politics at the theoretical level which will allow us to use the language of the common good. I pointed to Augustine's reaction to the claims of classical political theory on behalf of the state as moral educator. Augustine anticipated MacIntyre's critique to some extent, but also provided a way of seeing the limited good of temporal peace and justice as genuine goods and as the appropriate common good of the political community. I suggested the term 'public order' to mark this good. And finally, in showing the Aristotelian sources of my proposal, I am opening the way for an accommodation between an understanding of the common goods of cooperation and the achievements of liberal political institutions.

CHAPTER 5

ANOTHER LOOK AT PUBLIC ORDER

In my search for a theory which will enable us to explain cooperation in society I have moved beyond explanations based on the self-interest of individuals and looked at the goods of those involved in practices. This provided a clear example of common good, even if the vulnerability of practices to corruption in the direction of individuals pursuing their own interests was noted. The question is whether this understanding of common good, generated in terms of local, small-scale community, can provide a model for speaking of the modern state's large-scale cooperation in terms of the common good. My suggestion in the last chapter was that we have to understand the restricted horizon of the good which is the proper domain of the state as a subset of the unrestricted common good. This is consistent with the dual recognition that the state is not competent to be a moral educator and that the goods which it pursues are truly valuable. The restricted domain of the common good which is the proper object of the state has been labelled public order. This could be misleading, since this term may call to mind well-established characterisations of the role of the state. It is necessary, therefore, to distinguish my proposal from conventional definitions of public order. I will review a number of ideas which belong to the minimal agenda of the state as conceived of in the liberal tradition. There is first of all the issue of law and order, which is frequently identified with public order; secondly, the question of the protection which the state must accord to liberty; and thirdly, the responsibility of the state to be neutral in relation to the different visions of the human good. Each of these issues arises in liberal discussions of the role of the state, and either singly or jointly can be taken as identifying public order. My argument will be that these alone are insufficient even for characterising the domain of public order as a restricted element of the common good.

What is sought is a theoretical explanation of cooperation in society. But the more closely we approach actual political issues the clearer it becomes that the reasons offered in explanation can also function as arguments in favour of or against proposed policies. The distinction between the rationality articulated in the theory and the operative rationality in everyday life becomes difficult to sustain. Hence I start with a short dialogue in order to show the connection between the deliberations of citizens and the philosophers' theories. The imagined dialogue between a proponent of the minimal state and a sceptical citizen summarises the argument of the chapter. Insofar as the purpose of the state is understood to be confined to some limited objective, the state is qualified as minimal. The proponent (P) of the minimal state begins by suggesting

P: we need a strong state in order to ensure law and order, and everybody stands to benefit from the security provided.

The sceptical citizen (C) responds by saying

C: yes, of course we need law and order, but I am afraid of giving too much power to your strong state. We must limit the state's power some way, but how?

Following Mill the proponent might continue,

P: yes, state power must be limited, and individuals' liberty could be the basis for limiting state power, since people will want to be free to pursue their interests in the secure environment guaranteed by the state.

Again the sceptical citizen might respond by saying

C: yes, of course liberty must be protected, but people's actions are not simply their own affair, they often have considerable impact on others, which is not necessarily intended, and we would have to have some rational basis for restricting liberty.

P: That's a dangerous road for the state to take because if it tries to interfere in people's liberties, it will be favouring the goals and aspirations of some groups over those of others, and the state should remain neutral on those questions of the good.

The sceptic is unhappy with the assumption that the state could in fact be neutral and might reply by saying

C: the state inevitably favours some actions and forms of behaviour over others, and it inevitably encourages the training of citizens in particular civic virtues, so it does operate out of some conception of the good, however minimal. Therefore it is not neutral. Better then for it to articulate and defend the view of the human good on which it relies.

Such is the pattern of debate I see, and which I will present in greater detail in what follows. There are three issues: law and order, the protection of liberty, and neutrality in relation to different visions of the human good. There is in each case a proposition of a minimalist understanding of the common good of the political community, which cannot answer the concerns of the sceptical citizen. I will look at each of the arguments in the context of debates which have taken place on particular issues.

LAW AND ORDER

The challenge of terrorism and of political violence in recent decades in Ireland has given a special prominence to questions of the powers of the state and limits to those powers. Emergency legislation in both Ireland and the UK created special courts and gave additional powers to the respective police forces. Both the laws themselves, and the exercise of the additional powers by the executive and the judiciary, stimulated often heated debate and accusations of the violations of civil liberties. These debates raised questions about the role of the state in regard to law and order, and the limits to its powers. More recently, the revelation of major miscarriages of justice provoked reflection on the nature of the limits to the powers of the state and its agents.

One line of thought which permeates these discussions provides me with a clear example of a minimalist view of the role of the state. It is the argument that the state's function is to secure society against the threat of external or internal violence, and that to do so it must have the monopoly of force in its own hands. All the instruments of the state and its institutions are subordinate to this one goal so that even the law is to be understood as an instrument to be used to secure public order. This line of thought has a long pedigree going back to Thomas Hobbes's *Leviathan* but it also has its twentieth-century variants. The policies of national security which guided South and Central American states in their treatment of those who agitated for greater social justice and individual liberties came from this tradition. But also in Ireland and the UK those who expressed concern for civil liberties and natural justice because of the manner in which these states dealt with terrorists and their political supporters often found themselves arguing against this mind-set.

There have been many occasions on which agents of the state were accused of torture, or of implementing a shoot-to-kill policy, or of acting outside the law. On some of these occasions official backing for the accused officials seemed to imply that considerations of national security were allowed to override normal legal procedure and that the demands of the law were waived in such cases in which its application would jeopardise national interests. To many people this seemed to contradict the high moral tone in which adherence to the law is usually advocated by representatives of the state. The appearance of contradiction presumes a distinction between the moral demands of justice and of the law on the one hand, and public interest or national security on the other. This distinction has no place however in the strand of English

political thought deriving from Hobbes to which I am referring. This tradition will argue that public morality, law and
justice are instituted for the sake of security and for the public
interest. Since it is the responsibility of government to determine what is the public interest, and to legislate and apply law
accordingly, it is impossible by definition that the government's
action for the sake of the public interest could be criticised
on the basis of law. In practical terms, it is inconceivable that
the application of the law could be allowed to undermine its
purpose. This point of view is coherent only on the assumption
that there is no realm of natural justice or moral law, to which
those with the responsibilities of government must adhere,
other than their obligation to provide security for the citizen.[1]

The denial of the objectivity of moral values or precepts is a
fundamental tenet of the tradition of moral thought to which
I refer. An influential contemporary statement of an ethical
position consistent with this tradition is that presented by John
L. Mackie in two books on ethics, *Ethics: Inventing Right and
Wrong* and *Hume's Moral Theory*.[2] The first is mainly concerned
with a rejection of objectivity in morals. According to Mackie,
not only is positive law a human construct, but morality itself
is a product of human invention. Morality is a device whose
function is to make possible a minimum of security and
peaceful co-existence. Some such device is necessary, because
the spontaneous orientation towards competition and conflict
and the tension of divergent interests in human relations would
lead to social chaos, in the absence of some restraining order.
Accordingly, along with a negative thesis, that there are no
objective values which might serve as the basis of an objective
moral order, he asserts in a positive thesis that morality is a
device for achieving coordination in human affairs which are
characterised by a tendency to conflict.

Mackie's argument that morality is merely a useful construct
would seem to be at odds with the fact that it can only achieve
its purpose when people attribute objective validity to its values
or prescriptions. And in fact there is a widely held conviction
that the demands of morality have a validity beyond their social
usefulness. Mackie attempts to account for these facts in a

theory of objectification or projection. The moral features ascribed to actions or objects or institutions in moral statements are fictions, on his view. Only the moral sentiments of speakers are real. Moral sentiments are projected onto the actions or institutions under consideration, and then spoken of as if they were objective, and real features of the qualified objects. The pretence is to be maintained because of the usefulness of the institutions of morality and law for the regulation of social life. Since it is desired that people conform to the practices of morality and of law, these things are called good, and the obligations of the relevant prescriptions are qualified as having objective validity. Such qualifications are fictions, but they are useful fictions, and no one could have a justifiable reason for undermining their acceptance. Because without such fictions, the stability and security of social life would be jeopardised.

Throughout his two books on ethics, Mackie sees himself in line with the tradition from Hobbes and Hume. He finds fundamental agreement in this tradition on the negative and positive theses, namely in denying the existence of any objective moral qualities, and in seeing morality as a solution to social problems of partial conflict. However, Mackie generalises to the whole range of practical concerns what Hobbes discusses in relation to the political.

The conflict to which Thomas Hobbes addressed himself in his major work on political ideas, *Leviathan*, was typified by the English civil war. The experience of chaos throughout the 1640s, when neither king nor parliament was strong enough to guarantee peace and stable government, illustrates his fundamental question, namely, how to establish peaceful and harmonious civil society where the major threat to order is posed by the liberty of individuals, including religious fanatics. The condition of civil war was precisely what was to be expected, on Hobbes's view, whenever there was a collapse of authority in society. Where there is no common power strong enough to keep men in awe, as he would put it, people will relapse into their natural state, which is one of war of each against each. In the natural state, prior to their organisation in political society, people live in great insecurity and fear of one another. With no organised protection against those who would take advantage of them, but on the contrary plenty of reason and opportunity for one to attack or rob another, people must live in constant fear of their lives. Given the insecurity of these conditions, there would be none of the benefits now associated with life in society, agriculture, industry, trade, science and the arts. It is the institution of a civil authority capable of enforcing the peace which makes them possible.

In the state of nature as Hobbes conceives it, there is no moral law to regulate how people ought to behave, but each has total liberty to do whatever he thinks necessary to preserve his own life. Since the state of nature is a state of war, force and fraud are said to be the order of the day. There are no valid claims to property, there is no such thing as justice, until such time as there is a lawmaker who determines property claims, and what is right and wrong, just and unjust. Consideration of obligations towards others are only conceivable once a lawmaker has been instituted to determine those obligations and to enforce them.

Although the making of positive law introduces the categories of right and wrong, just and unjust, into social life, this is understood in such a way that it is by definition impossible to speak of the sovereign committing an injustice against a subject. The sovereign gives the law, but by definition is incapable of breaking the law. The sovereign is not a party to the original covenants which Hobbes understood as the origin of civil society. Those covenants are made by individuals with one another, agreeing to relinquish some of their liberty on condition that others do so too. Their additional promise to abide by the directives made by the common power constituted by the coalescence of their relinquished powers generates the sovereign. Formed by the coalescence of their individual powers, the sovereign is said to be authorised by the subjects. This means that the subjects admit themselves to be the authors of whatever is done by the sovereign in their name, and with their power. The consequences of this all-encompassing authorisation are enormous however. For it follows from this that the subjects are obliged to own and stand over whatever is done by the sovereign with their power and in their name for the sake of their peace and common defence. On this understanding, it is simply impossible that the sovereign could act unjustly in respect of any of the subjects. Hobbes explicitly denies that subjects could have grounds for criticising their sovereign's decisions or actions. There can be no restriction on the rights of the sovereign to do whatever he considers necessary in order to achieve the peace and security for which he was instituted.

Hobbes has little sympathy for those who would say that life under the rule of any such sovereign must be a highly unpleasant affair. He notes how the subjects of a monarchy complain about the inconveniences of that form of rule, and how the subjects of a democracy attribute all the inconveniences of their form of life to the democratic form of government. But Hobbes has little time for those supposed inconveniences. No matter how unpleasant submission to the rule of a sovereign might be, its disadvantages would be negligible in comparison with the total chaos which would ensue in the absence of an absolute, effective authority. No matter what complaints anyone might have against his sovereign, the grievance could not outweigh the advantages provided by a sovereign, namely in establishing a bulwark against the total chaos of civil war.

It is this mind-set which made possible the practices of torture on terrorist suspects, shoot-to-kill policies and a broad tolerance for infringements of regulations by members of the security forces. To challenge this position requires one to have some point of view on the human good which might be a basis for claims over against the state.

Objections to the abuse of state power are usually made in terms of rights. In the following chapters I will explore the language of rights especially in relation to liberty, and I will examine the usefulness of this language for handling problems located in the relationship of the state to the human good. At this point, I merely wish to underline the unsatisfactoriness of a position which makes the law and order issue the only issue

84   *A Politics of the Common Good*

for the state and which places no limits on the actions which may be done by the state and its agencies for the sake of that minimal common good.

THE PROTECTION OF LIBERTY

An unrestricted state power is definitely threatening since one would have no protection against arbitrary use of that power. There is a need to limit power and the search for the basis of appropriate limits has led people to the idea of liberty. State power was seen to pose a major threat to individuals' freedom of action and the advocate of liberty wants to ensure that such enormous power is kept within limits. The approach which wants to restrict state power in the name of liberty also tends to be minimalist in its determination of the role of the state, even if it is at the opposite pole to the law and order emphasis.

THE DISTINCTIONS OF LIBERTY

Liberty is frequently distinguished into negative and positive liberty, freedom from, and freedom to.[3] As a philosophical and political movement in the modern period, liberalism has focused primarily on negative liberty. The need was to protect the freedoms of individuals against the all-embracing power of autocratic states and dogmatic orthodoxies. And because states and orthodoxies, including religious orthodoxies, expressly espoused some idea of what would be for the good of people, and what would allow them to be truly free, any positive version of liberty was suspect as a threat to negative liberty. Liberty, negatively understood, was asserted over against tyrannical, autocratic or paternalistic power.

Michael Novak has usefully distinguished the three types of liberation which were sought, calling them the political, the economic and the cultural.[4] Those committed to the defence of liberty sought to create institutions which would secure a space for individuals to act, free from interference by representatives of power. Against the background of experience of tyrannical government which resorted to torture and direct coercion, liberals like John Locke sought the creation of limited government, bound in its power by the constitutional protection of the rights including liberties of individuals, bound to seek the consent of the governed in democratic process, and limited also by the separation of powers in the state. This has been the agenda of political liberation. Economic freedoms were sought against the background of unwelcome taxation and the restrictions imposed on trade by mercantalist policy; these restrictions were seen to hinder the creation of wealth and the overcoming of problems of poverty. Those who argued for the free market like Adam Smith pointed to the greater advantages which economic liberties would bring to the wealth of the nation. And thirdly, the demand for moral and cultural liberation was made against a background of censorship of publications and oppression of consciences. Religious liberty, freedom of speech, a free press and the separation of church and state were the appropriate institutional arrangements to ensure that individuals would be free from state coercion in this dimension of their lives. John Stuart Mill was a particular champion of the freedom of speech and thought.

Even allowing for the complexity of the liberty sought with its different levels, the pursuit of liberty was largely defensive. The aspiration to freedom to pursue the truth and engage in unrestricted public discussion, to own and produce and trade in goods without interference, and to participate in the government of one's country without fear was nourished and grew in the experience of its opposite. The familiar threats to liberty in the form of coercive state power, centralised control of the economy and censorship of speech and thought made clear what needed to be defended: a protected space in which individuals could speak and act freely in pursuit of their own chosen purposes.

Mill on Liberty

John Stuart Mill was a key advocate for this space. His 1859 essay *On Liberty* is widely regarded as a landmark statement of the importance of freedom for the well-being of individuals. Unless a person has some scope to decide for himself what he wants to achieve and some opportunity to act freely in pursuit of those goals, he cannot achieve that self-development which Mill along with other Enlightenment thinkers identified as an essential good. No other benefits provided for him by the choice and action of others could compensate for the lack of freedom to act. So convinced is Mill of this that he rules out even a benign paternalism as a ground for limiting the freedom of another. As he formulates it in his famous principle:

> The object of this Essay is to assert *one very simple principle*, as entitled to govern absolutely the dealings of society with the individual in the way of compulsion and control, whether the means used be physical force in the form of legal penalties, or the moral coercion of public opinion. That principle is, that *the sole end* for which mankind are warranted, individually or collectively, in interfering with the liberty of action of any of their number, is self-protection. That *the only purpose* for which power can be rightfully exercised over any member of a civilised community, against his will, is to prevent harm to others.[5]

On closer reading, this apparently clear principle appears to be rather more complex, if not confused. The basic point is clear: individuals are to be allowed freedom to act, but with an exception. That exception is marked in the two key sentences by the words 'sole end' and 'only purpose'; but the end and purpose identified are not the same: the sole end of self-protection differs from the only purpose of protection of others. Further, it is not clear who or what those 'others' are, and who is entitled to impose limits on individuals' action when it threatens the well-being of others. What it is for an individual to protect himself is clear; but is Mill allowing for individuals in society to restrict the liberties of others when they judge them to be threatening? Self-protection is also allowed to society in addition to individuals; but in what sense can the actions of individuals pose a threat to society? Are individuals entitled to restrict the liberties of some to protect others, or is it only society or the state which may so act? How are we to interpret the phrase 'mankind . . . individually or collectively'? And if we agree on this principle as a basis for limiting freedom, do we have to agree that it is the *only* principle?

Mill's very simple principle is not so simple after all.[6] Nevertheless, it expresses an important truth: that the freedom of individuals is to be respected, and not to be constrained without appropriate reason. Liberty is a moral claim imposing limits on what the state can legitimately do to people. It is commitment to this which makes one a liberal. Liberals can find themselves in disagreement with one another on some of the open questions left by Mill's statement. There can be disagreement on whether and how and how much certain actions of individuals pose a threat to society; there can be disagreement on the role of the state and its law in protecting society as well as individual others. These questions are not settled by reaching agreement on the basic point of the value of liberty.

LIBERALISM WITHOUT RELATIVISM

A common misapprehension is that a commitment to the principle of liberty implies relativism. The line of thought is in three steps: liberty involves freedom of speech; freedom of speech cultivates a pluralism of viewpoints; pluralism is always linked to relativism. Perhaps it is not surprising if the opponents of liberalism make the accusation of relativism, but it is an abandonment of the cause when the defenders of liberty espouse relativism as a linked doctrine. Lest the plethora of *isms* confuse matters, let me clarify what I mean. The point is illustrated in a familiar cliché in public comment: 'well he would say that, wouldn't he?' The content of whatever is said, be it by someone in public office or a spokesperson for business or church or some organisation, is not considered. The arguments which might be brought forward to substantiate that content are ignored. It is sufficient to remark on the position of the speaker, in the words of another cliché, to locate 'where he is coming from', in order to dismiss the speaker's contribution. This is relativism in practice: the doctrine that opinions derive their validity from the standpoint of their holder, and that something is only true *for* persons who hold it to be true. It is understandable that the recognition of a plurality of viewpoints would be associated with a relativist doctrine that one viewpoint is as good as any other from the perspective of truth. But there is no necessity that the two be linked, and it would be contradictory to the liberalism of J. S. Mill so to link them.

Mill insisted on allowing freedom of opinion and freedom of expression, not because all opinions were equally valid, but because the only way to arrive at the truth of some matter was to allow open and unrestricted debate on all relevant questions. He warned against suppressing any opinion, which, if the opinion turned out to be right, would amount to a suppression of the truth. And even if the suppressed opinion were mistaken, an opportunity would have been lost to clarify the correct position and to make the error evident. Mill wanted to protect the space for freedom of expression, so that a plurality of opinions would be subject to the testing of public debate, and progress might be made in identifying warranted positions and abandoning the mistaken. For Mill the point was not that people should be allowed the freedom to *have* opinions, but that people would have the freedom to *do* something appropriate with their opinion, namely, present and defend it in public debate, and modify or retain or abandon it as rational argument requires.[7] Of course, rational argument is not always conclusive, and so there must be tolerance of conflicting opinions, so that the truth can be pursued. Tolerance has an instrumental value: it is subordinate to the goal of truth. This liberal position of Mill is not the same as the predominant contemporary demand for toleration for differing opinions, to be tolerated simply because they are *held* by some, without a requirement that they be presented for public scrutiny and debate.

The 'Harm to Others' Principle Including Harm to Society

Another of the confusing ambiguities in Mill's principle has to do with the question of who is to be protected from harm. There is one rather simple reading of the text which sees the state in the role of boxing referee whose job it is to ensure that the boxers abide by the rules and do not harm one another beyond what the rules allow. The principle then is read as a warning to the referee not to overstep his due authority. It is as if only the combatants themselves are in danger of being harmed. Of course, we know from the world of sport that the referee too can be injured, that his authority can be undermined, that the sport of boxing itself can be brought into ill-repute by the behaviour of its participants, and that the standards of sportsmanship can decline. There are other harms possible, beyond those which the contestants inflict on one another. And correspondingly in social life, there are damages inflicted which undermine authority, which weaken social cohesion and which lower standards of public behaviour. Are these covered by Mill's principle? His formulation seems to allow the interpretation that they are. He concedes that mankind collectively can be warranted in interfering with the freedom of action of someone in the case of self-protection. That is, in protection of the collective, social good. The threat of harm to society as such may be included therefore within the ambit of the principle.

Although this is a plausible reading consistent with the text, Mill's principle is usually applied only to the cases of individuals harming others. This is consistent with the prevalent tendency to analyse social relations in terms of individuals only. However, it is no less an authentic application of the liberal concern to see it as including the well-being of society also. The prevalent blindness to the social can be noted in recent Irish experience. In the controversial debates on the issues of law and morality, there is often a reluctance to conduct debate in terms of the 'harm to others' aspect of proposals. As an instance of such reluctance consider the remarks made by sociologist Michele Dillon in her study of the debate on divorce in 1986, *Debating Divorce: Moral Conflict in Ireland.*[8] She reports the arguments presented by the Catholic bishops in their pastoral letter *Love is for Life* and by the main spokespersons for the Anti-Divorce Campaign, William Binchy and Joe McCarroll, as focusing on social and economic aspects of divorce law. She acknowledges that these arguments were constructed to make the point that a change in the law would result in greater harm both to society as a whole and to individual women and children who were likely to be victims. Whatever may have been the validity of those arguments, they did at least conceivably fall under Mill's rubric of 'harm to others'. This would have been the test as proposed by Mill for the acceptability of laws restricting personal freedoms. Dillon does not report if or how those arguments were refuted, but offers her own comment that these protagonists really opposed divorce for reasons of a moral nature which they were not prepared to admit.

CONCLUSION

The sceptical citizen in our fictitious dialogue would be willing to adopt the liberal position, if the term liberal is understood in a sense consistent with Mill's principle, that state power should not be used to restrict human liberty except where the exercise of that liberty involves harm to others. Harm to others would have to be understood broadly as including harm to society. Also with Mill the sceptical citizen would advocate tolerance of a plurality of opinions, so that open public discussion of those opinions would lead to a sifting out of the truth from indefensible positions. A doctrine of relativism is dangerous because a prevalence of this doctrine would affect one aspect of public order, namely, the understanding of public debate as oriented to attaining the truth, or at least eroding falsehood.

NEUTRALITY ON THE GOOD?

The imagined dialogue between the proponent of a minimal state and a sceptical citizen might now move on to the topic of the state's neutrality in relation to substantive accounts of the human good. The suggestion that individuals' liberties might be restricted by law for the sake of public order or the common good usually provokes anxiety on the part of those who wish to protect liberty from state interference. While it is conceded that the law may have to restrict the liberty of some in order to protect the liberty of others, it is also strongly argued that the possibility of the law favouring the interests of some groups over those of others must be avoided strenuously. This is a traditionally liberal concern. I will first of all present the liberal position on the relationship between the law and the common good. Secondly, I turn to the writings of Frederick Hayek to exemplify the abhorrence at arbitrariness, which a liberal legal system is explicitly designed to avoid. Thirdly, I suggest that in the terms in which the problem is posed, it will be impossible to avoid arbitrariness, and that the very attempt to achieve neutrality in making and applying law obliges us to raise again the question of the human good.

THE LAW AND THE GOOD

As discussed in Chapter 4, there is a spectrum of possible views on the proper relationship of politics and the law to the question of the human good. The spectrum is stretched between two poles. On the one hand there are various positions which recognise some good as the purpose of politics, and by derivation of the law. These positions are frequently of Aristotelian ancestry, although they may not share Aristotle's view of the good life. On this view, political discourse itself is the debate about the good life, about the kind of life which is worth living and which the political community would like to achieve for itself. Politics is the search for common purposes, for a life appropriate to the dignity of the human subject. On this view the existence of diversity of opinions enriches the debate, and the political process is the struggle to get an answer and to realise it. The law at any time is the product of the discourse at whatever stage it has reached, and necessarily encapsulates a vision of the good life in a manner appropriate to the law.

At the other extreme are positions which insist that political authority and the law must be neutral between differing and competing visions of the good. Insofar as the law can be said to have a purpose, it is to arbitrate between persons and groups which come into conflict with one another because the purposes which they set themselves are incompatible. So the law's purpose is not any good as such, but the protection and facilitation of those who in their pursuit of their own vision of their good constitute a threat to one another. Hence the tradition of the securing of liberties to the point at which they threaten the liberties of others. The disagreement about the human good and the fact of diversity in visions of the human good provide the political community and the law with the task of maintaining a minimum of public order such that the liberties of each to pursue his view of the good is not impeded by others who hold contrary views. The liberal understanding of the law is that it provides a basis for public order which no view of the good is capable of providing.[9]

This liberal view relies on the premise that the question of the good is unanswerable. The good is said to be a matter of taste, or religious belief, or of philosophical conviction, and as such it is beyond argument. A fully stated position such as Mackie's, which I discussed above, may include the statement that values are not objective, and that morality is a fiction. In Hobbes's famous phrase, 'that which men desire is what they call good'. Goods are the objects of individuals' desires, but there cannot be any objective good, or objective value. In the context of incompatible purposes and differing conceptions of the good, the law may not be allowed arbitrate on the question of what is truly good and rely on any such conclusion for its decisions. On this view of law, any judgement which seems to favour one vision of the good will either have to accept the criticism of arbitrariness, or admit the question of the good as a legitimate question.

HAYEK ON ARBITRARINESS

Hayek is a well-known defender of individual liberty, especially in economic matters.[10] He is an advocate for the rule of law in order to protect liberty against arbitrariness. He argues that the primary role of a liberal constitution is to protect and secure individual liberty. Historically, liberty was asserted over against the discretionary authority of rulers, and this background still influences the definition of the concept: liberty is

   . . . the possibility of a person's acting according to his own decisions and plans, in contrast to the position of one who was irrevocably subject to the will of another who by arbitrary decision could coerce him to act or not to act in specific ways. The time-honoured phrase by which this freedom has often been described is therefore 'independence of the arbitrary will of another'.[11]

Examples of 'the arbitrary will of another' can easily be found in the accounts of autocratic rulers known from history. However, Hayek is not only warning about the danger of such individuals or groups attaining political power. 'Arbitrary' means action determined by a particular will unrestrained by a general rule, irrespective of whether this will is of one or a majority. Arbitrary rule would arise whenever legislators would allow particular cases or particular interests to influence the formulation of law. Only if people are subject to general rules is their liberty protected under the rule of law. The key to the rule of law, and hence to the protection of liberty, is the generality of the rules by which life in society is to be regulated. The greatest threat to liberty and to the undermining of the rule of law arises whenever that generality which ought to characterise the law is diminished. Such threats are frequent according to Hayek, especially because every act of the legislature now qualifies as law. It is often assumed that the majority view is necessarily just and cannot be arbitrary, but Hayek challenges this naive assumption.[12] Arbitrary power, enforcing its edicts to the injury of persons and property of its subjects, is not law, whether manifested as the decree of a personal monarch or of an impersonal multitude.[13]

The rule of law excludes in principle certain kinds of governmental measures, because they involve arbitrary discrimination between persons. Whenever the law has to make distinctions, and name particular subgroups, the danger arises of arbitrariness creeping into the laws. Either privilege or discrimination, which are forms of arbitrary selection, can arise whenever distinctions are drawn between groups of people, such that the good of one group will be subject to the will of another.[14]

Hayek makes his case for individual liberty and for its protection in the rule of law, not in support of existing regimes, but in criticism of the tyranny of majorities characteristic of contemporary political systems. He argues that because governments in democracies need majorities, and majorities are usually composed of coalitions of interest groups, those in power must purchase support by catering for the interests of marginal groups in the coalition. As a result, law is anything but general. In an unlimited democracy, the holders of discretionary powers are forced to use them, whether they wish it or not, to favour particular groups.[15] The majority, in order to remain the majority, must use its power for this purpose. The legislative assembly, which should serve as a protection against arbitrary power, is driven to take control of all spheres of life. Hayek's conclusion, writing in a British context, is that parliament is now the greatest threat to liberty. Parliament is now almighty, so that the free constitution now means a licence to the majority in parliament to act as arbitrarily as it pleases.[16]

> The effective limitation of power is the most important problem of social order. Government is indispensable for the formation of such an order only to protect all against coercion and violence from others. But as soon as, to achieve this, government successfully claims the monopoly of coercion and violence, it becomes also the chief threat to individual freedom.[17]

> I trust there will come a time when people will look with the same horror at the idea of a body of men, even one authorised by a majority of the citizens, who possess power to order whatever it likes, as we feel today about most other forms of authoritarian government.[18]

The Problems of Order and Freedom

Hayek's writings highlight the confidence placed by liberal thought in the possibility of impartial law providing a solution to the key problems of order and freedom. The issue of how the endemic hostility in social life can be controlled is the problem of order. How are restraints to be imposed on mutual antagonism so as to ensure the satisfaction of mutual need? Restraints will inevitably restrict the pursuit by some of their desired goals. The problem of freedom is the question of how order can be instituted without giving undue preference to the goals of some or arbitrarily depriving others of their good.

How can order be instituted in such a way that no one's liberty is unjustifiably preferred or downgraded and that everyone has the largest amount of liberty compatible with the absence of such arbitrariness?[19] The single solution offered for these two problems in liberal thought is the application of impersonal laws. But how are such laws to be made, and how is their content to be determined?

As we have seen in Chapter 2, an appeal to the self-interest of each participant has its problems. It is in an individual's own interest to benefit from a system of laws established by others, but not to obey or establish that system himself.[20] Alternatively, appeal to values which are actually shared is also unsatisfactory. After all, it is the assumption of the liberal analysis that we have to resort to a set of public rules as the foundation of order and freedom because it is accepted that there cannot be rational agreement on values.[21] There might be factual agreement among members of a group as to what is of value, but such sharing of values is contingent, and cannot be normative. So what hope is there of finding a solution to the problem? In what follows, I want to look at two related issues in which the problem of arbitrariness and impartiality arises, namely the issues of licensing embryo research in the UK, and abortion in Ireland.

Embryo Research

The Warnock Report provides us with a concrete example of the issues addressed above. This was the report of a committee called to make proposals about the need for law to regulate experimentation on human embryos. In her introduction to the *Report* Mary Warnock identifies the locus of the question addressed by the committee as the relationship between law and morality.[22] She proceeds to discuss the difficulties of identifying what are in fact the demands of morality, and the need for sensitivity to the feelings of people. She concludes that the law must 'be drawn with a view to the common good, however this notoriously imprecise goal is to be identified.'[23] In the foreword to the *Report* itself, the committee undertook 'to discover the public good, in the widest sense'.[24] The law to be drawn up would be 'the embodiment of a common moral position', 'a broad framework for what is morally acceptable within society'.[25] The question is said to boil down to the issue of what kind of society is desirable.

Mary Warnock dismissed the suggestion that there might be a committee of moral experts to decide on the issues addressed. Her reason for taking this stance was that she did not think it possible to form a correct judgement on such moral matters: 'It cannot be too strongly emphasised that in questions of morality, though there may be better and worse judgements, there is no such thing as a correct judgement'.[26] Moral theories could not solve the issue for the committee, because the issue of the status of the embryonic life would have to be settled before any moral theory might be applied.

Turning from theory to popular sentiment, the committee failed to find an unambiguous indication for policy. The problem which they faced reflected a contradiction in the value judgements of society, because society was found to value things which are incompatible with each other. 'Society as a whole values advances in science, especially in medicine; . . . But the research upon which such advances depend seems to run counter to another highly prized value, the absolute sanctity of human life from its earliest stage of development'.[27] The committee identified here an incompatibility if not contradiction in the values of society. Majority and minority on the committee differed on the question whether the sanctity of human life in general could be upheld if very early embryos were used in research. And so it was seen to be a matter for the legislators to decide which value to place higher.

As a veteran of such committees, Mary Warnock was eager to achieve some measure of consensus even though it was clear that not all points of view could be accommodated. There would have to be a proposal formulated which could find acceptance among people, at least to the extent of not provoking popular outrage. But as she explained, the acceptance generated would not be based on a correct theory or judgement. It would be a matter of testing the proposal's compatibility with widespread feeling among citizens.

This was indeed a difficult matter requiring legislation, but therefore a useful test case to examine the capabilities of the liberal understanding of law in handling conflict. The Warnock Committee reiterated this liberal understanding, reflecting many of the points made by Hayek: the law must be definite in a conflict situation;[28] it must be general, uniform, public[29] and enforceable.[30] The law must not violate liberty;[31] it must protect the weak, those likely to come off worse in conflict of interests with the powerful.[32] The law is an embodiment of a common moral position in society, expressing limits in a pluralist society, in which many differing views of the good are held.[33] But despite this nuanced understanding of the law and its function, the proposal about what the law should be in this one case of conflict appealed to political viability, measured in terms of popular sentiment and reaction. But since it is also maintained that values are subjective, then the common moral position of society which is to be reflected in the law is merely a contingent agreement. The foundations for the law are sentiments, which happen to be held by sufficient numbers of people.

> Society feels, albeit obscurely, that its members, especially the most helpless, such as children and the very old, must be protected against possible exploitation by enthusiastic scientists; and embryos are brought into the category of those deserving protection, just as animals are. This is a matter of public, and widely shared, *sentiment.*[34]

And the absence of 'absolute outrage of general moral sentiment' was one of the conditions on which the majority on the committee would permit experimentation on embryos less than fourteen days old.[35]

I suggest that this is a case of the arbitrariness which Hayek identifies as the greatest threat to liberty. It also illustrates the arbitrariness in giving preference to the values of some in the determinations of the law, which contradicts the very nature of the law as neutral between competing notions of the good. The law is made to depend on head-counting ultimately, and so instead of protecting liberty against discretionary power, it is in danger of favouring another kind of tyranny, the tyranny of the majority. From this examination of one contemporary issue, the sceptical citizen may query the real possibility of neutrality on the part of the law and the state in relation to the competing comprehensive views of the good held by citizens.

ABORTION AS A QUESTION OF RECOGNITION

A pluralist society demands a liberal democracy, that is, a political system in which a variety of views of what constitutes a good life is not only tolerated but fostered. With the emphasis on liberal as a qualifier of democracy, such a system abhors any attempt to impose by law a particular view of the good on people. And yet the law will restrict people's scope of action in order to protect the freedom of others, and to maintain the conditions which will allow each person or group to pursue their own vision of the good life.

Accordingly, a pluralist society will be very sensitive to any attempt to deny a minority or particular group the opportunity of pursuing the good as they see it. That anyone might possibly be excluded arbitrarily from such a society and the protection it offers is likely to arouse indignation. And should anyone appropriate to themselves the entitlement to decide who may enjoy the freedoms guaranteed in this society and who may not, they will be subjected to the most rigorous demands for justification. While such a system will always require officers and institutions with authority to sanction, no one group or point of view may dictate the policy to be followed in terms of their own preferred vision of the good. Because of its commitment to the protection of liberty, a pluralist society will be very careful about all those instances in which it is decided who is to be recognised as entitled to protection and who not.

That is why abortion is a critical issue for a pluralist society. It challenges those committed to the idea of individual freedom to take a stance on the question of recognition: who is to be recognised as entitled to protection, and who not? Usually, debates about abortion focus on two issues: first, the status of the unborn, whether it is the sort of thing which may not be killed, a human being, entitled to respect; and, second, women's rights, whether their freedom is to be respected to the extent of allowing them to have the choice in regard to abortions. Both issues are crucial for a society which aspires to protect freedoms and to limit freedoms only when necessary.

Precisely because it would be highly sensitised to the problems of exclusion, a pluralist society might be expected to show extreme caution in regard to abortion. Because, even if the state wanted to remain neutral on the question of the good, it cannot remain neutral on the first issue in the debate, the status of the unborn. The possibility at least must be faced that abortion might well be the taking of human life. The issue at stake is not a matter of a debatable view of the good, but a case of recognition or exclusion. The state cannot be neutral on who is recognised and who is excluded. It may decide to recognise the unborn as entitled to protection, or it may exclude the unborn from the protection it offers; there is no third, neutral position. The endorsement of a policy which made abortion available might well be a serious violation of a fundamental principle of liberal democracy, namely, that the rights and freedoms of human beings are to be protected.[36] And furthermore, the state's acknowledgement of women's rights in the matter of abortion might well be more than a case of the respect to be shown to individual liberty and privacy. It might also be an instance of the delegation of the power to decide who is to enjoy the recognition and the protection of the state, and who is to be excluded. But precisely the question of recognition could never be a private matter in a liberal democracy which remained faithful to its principles of respect for individual freedom and neutrality in relation to visions of the good. Although women are indeed directly affected by abortion, it would be as intolerable for the state to hand over to them the exercise of its power of recognition or exclusion as to any other *private* person or group.

Abortion is a crucial issue for a liberal democracy in a pluralist society. It is crucial, because insofar as it raises the questions of recognition, of who is to be entitled to the protection of the law, and who is to be entitled to recognise or exclude, it addresses the basic principles which such a society claims for itself. A liberal democracy in a pluralist society must be decisive on the issues of recognition and exclusion, and it must retain the power of decision on these matters in the public sphere, withdrawing them from the realm of private choice. For this reason it is not at all inappropriate that the constitution of a state which claimed for itself the qualities of a liberal democracy should make a statement in relation to the recognition of the unborn, even though it is totally inappropriate that a state should rely on the wording of its constitution for effective criminal law. Article 40.3.3 of the Constitution of Ireland, recognising the unborn as entitled to the protection of the law, is placed in the context of Article 40 in which the state's obligation to protect the rights of every citizen is acknowledged. The Eighth Amendment is consistent with liberal democratic principles in giving recognition to the unborn, and in withdrawing the matter from the realm of private choice.

Hannah Arendt has argued that politics in the modern world has evolved into a public handling of essentially domestic matters.[37] By this she means that the concerns of the household in sustaining and reproducing life have become the business of politics. The economy, the provision of jobs, the stabilisation of the currency, the balancing of the budget, all these matters which in the classical world were considered to belong to the private domain of the household have become the agenda of contemporary politics. As a result, the issues which engaged the minds of citizens in the (admittedly idealised) Greek *polis*, questions concerning the good life and the moral qualities of citizens and their institutions, are now deemed to be matters of private opinion. If such a development is regrettable as Arendt suggests, Ireland can at least boast that in its modern political culture debates on issues of the good and the good life have been kept on the top of the agenda. The focus of public concern has not been confined to survival, life itself, but has embraced the moral issues pertaining to the good life.

CONCLUSION

In this chapter I have explored a number of ideas in relation to the minimal agenda of a liberal state. Through the lens of an imaginary dialogue I have reflected on three issues: the topic of law and order, the limitation of state power in terms of liberty, and the neutrality of the state in relation to disputes about the good. Each of the positions on the limited role of the state can be understood as a possible delineation of the restricted common good which is the proper object of politics, namely, public order. However, on each issue questions were identified which could not be answered in terms of the minimal ideas alone, and which pointed to the need for a broader vocabulary for specifying the common good of liberal politics.

It may seem that I have moved altogether from a consideration of theories of cooperation to the rhetoric of political debate. Each of the possible versions of public order was discussed in the context of issues which have been part of public controversy in the recent past. Some of these issues can still engage us emotionally and provoke us to enter debate directly on behalf of our favoured position. My aim has been to show how positions taken up in these debates reflect particular views of the purpose of the state. In particular, I have argued that concern for law and order, the protection of liberty, and neutrality in relation to the good imply positions on public order. These positions may remain implicit or they may be articulated in elaborate presentations. Whichever is the case, the positions adopted are prescriptive, expressing what ought to be the case and what the speaker would wish to have realised in his own situation. The articulation of what is appropriate and good and desirable is typical of such encounters as that imagined at the beginning of the chapter between the advocate of the minimal state and the sceptical citizen. My concern now is to draw the connection between the language of advocacy typical of political debate, and the language of explanation to be relied upon in understanding human cooperation. In advocating certain institutions and structures as in the imaginary dialogue, people rely on a language which is normative and prescriptive. This is appropriate, because they are arguing for what they want. But then, when it comes to explaining the very institutions or structures which were the product of previous debates, the expectation conditioned by our dominant model of science is that the language of explanation would be purely descriptive. For instance, the theoretical models which attempt to explain social interaction in terms of self-interest present themselves as descriptive. I suggest that they merely appear to be descriptive, precisely because the prescriptive elements which belonged in the contexts in which they originated are conveniently forgotten.

Hobbes, Mill and Hayek can provide examples from the preceding discussion. These three served as spokesmen for the three possible versions of public order. Each of them wrote as an advocate, wanting to persuade readers about the best form of state given their situations.[38] Each of them wrote in the context of conflict. Accordingly, each attempts to appeal to reasons equally accessible to all parties in the conflict. And so Hobbes assumes that all are equally interested in survival and security, Mill assumes that all will want to have as much freedom of action as possible, and Hayek assumes that no one will want to have his opponents' interests favoured in preference to his own. I noted above in the discussion of altruism in Chapter 3 that this kind of search for common ground is typical of situations of conflict and can generate powerful philosophical tools which may be of use in helping conflicted parties come to some arrangement. When the philosophical tools are divorced from the originating context, however, they appear to be autonomous explanatory models and the assumptions on which they are based are generalised beyond the situations of conflict. I discussed this tendency in the first chapter in relation to the explanation of punishment and the application of Hobbes's ideas in that context.

In a conflict situation, the search for common ground may prove fruitful. However, what common ground may be found in any particular conflict situation cannot be anticipated, and must be established from experience. It seems dogmatic to dictate in advance what alone may serve as common ground. Why need it be restricted to the ideas considered above, namely security to ensure survival, liberty to pursue one's interests, and assurance that the state will not give preference to one's opponents' interests? The arguments presented by the sceptical citizen in the dialogue, and by myself in the discussion, point to a broader horizon within which common ground may be sought and indeed found. That horizon includes some questions concerning the human good since the liberal state cannot achieve the desired neutrality on the good; it includes some questions concerning the public good since that is also seen as a reason for restricting the liberties of individuals; and it includes questions concerning the limits to what the state may do to people in the name of law and order. To this list we could also add from the discussion in the last chapter the institutions which either immediately or remotely foster and sustain the practices within which people pursue internal goods and their visions of the good life.

Where agreement either exists or can be created in relation to such common ground in the context of conflict, then those elements on which agreement is reached are common goods of those involved. They are common to participants as part of what each wants, even if only as condition for achieving their other goals. As I argued in the previous chapter, it is appropriate to use the term common good in this context also. To link these elements of the common good under the term public order emphasises that they belong to the restricted domain of the common good which is the appropriate field of influence of the state, and do not exhaust the common good of humanity as such.

Chapter 6

RIGHTS AND PUBLIC ORDER

In conflict situations it makes sense to try to find common ground on which to build an agreement, and since conflict situations arise because parties do not agree, the possible range of common ground is limited. Hence the restricted nature of the candidates for agreement which I considered in the last chapter, namely, the guarantee of security, the protection of liberty, and the non-interference by the state in the debate on the good. If conflict is taken to be the context of modern politics, then the basis of agreement on what the nature and purpose of the state should be must seem to be equally restricted. In the previous chapter I argued that the minimalist descriptions of public order, the purpose of the state, need not be taken in the sense in which they are often presented, namely, as dogmatic *a priori* statements of what alone the state should do. Other questions indicated the possibility of an even broader base consistent with the values of law and order, liberty, and respect for differences of view on the human good. Those questions pointed to the still outstanding task of charting the domain of public order. For instance, if Mill's principle is interpreted to include the defence of society, as I suggested, what are the social goods which must be protected? As a first step in charting at least in outline the domain of public order I will discuss the language of rights. This discussion should provide some illustration of the thrust of my argument. It is appropriate at this point, because on the one hand, the listing of rights is frequently taken as a way of establishing the limited common ground which exists between conflicting parties, and on the other hand, it is not possible to specify rights without some consideration of the human good. Further, consideration of the role of the state and the law in regard to rights allows for a clearer focus on what I mean by the domain of public order.

Public debate on controversial issues today is usually formulated in the language of rights. This language is particularly rich. The complexity and ambiguity of the concept of rights allow for the expression of a great range of nuances and meanings. On the other hand, it is attractive as a language for debating purposes because it appears to offer conclusive directions in complicated situations. The assertion of rights, which is so much part of political debate in our world, derives its popularity from its success in course of the Enlightenment. Although ultimately derived from the usage of the ancient Roman courts, the language of rights was shaped and established as the appropriate medium for political debate in the struggles to win freedoms from autocratic rulers and oppressive or at least authoritative systems of rule at the birth of the modern period. Those who coined and fashioned the language of rights, especially John Locke, Immanuel Kant, Thomas Paine, and the thinkers of the French Revolution, were all engaged in political struggles to secure civil liberties against the arbitrary exercise of power by kings who would claim absolute authority as their justification. The appeal to human rights was made to indicate a limitation on royal power, and to assert a moral reality which the sovereign too should respect. Our modern vocabulary of rights was forged in the context of the English (1688), American (1776) and French (1789) revolutions. And in this context, the predominant concern of those who asserted human rights was to secure liberties for individual citizens against the arbitrary exercise of royal power. Thomas Hobbes too, although he argued the case for an absolute sovereign, shaped the subsequent language of rights on the anvil of the question of how much liberty might be allowed to individuals without jeopardising public order. The contemporary vocabulary of rights, and the manner in which this language is used today, reflect this origin in political conflict and in the desire to safeguard liberties.

In all the recent Irish debates on matters of law and morality participants spontaneously stated their case in terms of rights, for example the right to life of the unborn, the right to control over what happens in and to one's body, the right to divorce, minorities' rights to liberties which do not threaten the preferred lifestyle of the majority, the right to privacy, the right to travel, the right to information. Each new issue brings a crop of newly asserted rights. The most recent eruption of the language of rights in the headlines has been the campaign for animal rights. This event in itself reveals how malleable is the language of rights. The rhetoric of rights in such debates seems to rely on an assertion of a moral claim which seeks recognition in the law. The focus in debate is usually on this connection between moral rights and legal entitlements, and that is understandable because the point of debate is frequently an attempt to change the law. However, little attention is paid to the basis on which moral rights are asserted, or to the question of how moral rights are known. Consistent with the heritage of the human rights tradition, it is taken for granted that such rights are self-evident. However, the experience of debate shows that the rights asserted on both sides of any dispute are frequently incompatible and seemingly irreconcilable, but they are asserted nevertheless in such a way that no compromise or limitation on the right could be accepted, for example the unborn child's right to life and the mother's right to choose. This experience of the interminability of debate raises the question of the basis of rights and how we know what they are. In order to handle this question of the basis and meaning of moral rights, it would seem necessary to enter into the debate on what is good for people. But since there are differing and competing visions of the human good, we can also expect disagreements on what are moral rights. The language available for conducting this debate between differing accounts of the human good cannot be that of rights, since the point is to establish what rights are to be recognised.

WHY THE SPONTANEOUS RESORT TO RIGHTS LANGUAGE?

The language of rights is legal in origin.[1] The language of law and rights used in the moral domain is borrowed from the experience of civil law, which is characterised by the possibility of having claims adjudicated and decisions enforced. This language is very useful for expressing the conclusions of practical arguments and the resolution of actual conflict. This is the model we are familiar with from courts of law. A judge or a jury determines an issue, putting an end to the conflict, terminating it, by declaring which of the parties in dispute is within their rights.[2] Those rights are secured for people by the relevant body of law.

Not all disputes can be resolved in such a manner. Political debate is not so much focused on who is within her legal rights, but on what those rights should be. In the rhetoric of political debate the proponents of an argument will spontaneously tend to present their demands in terms of rights, of rights to be secured in law, to be respected and allowed exercise without unnecessary limitation. Presuming good will, each side in a dispute is convinced of the correctness of its case, and demands the securing of its asserted rights with moral assurance.

In those public debates which are concerned with what the law should be, and what rights should be secured in law, the tendency is to argue in terms of moral rights which ought to be secured in legal rights. This is well illustrated in the recent debates on the constitutional referenda: the right to life of the unborn, the woman's right to control what may happen in and to her body, the right to divorce, the rights of minorities, and so on. Couching such arguments in the language of rights lends them an air of plausibility and confers on them an authority which is commonly associated with the authoritative determinations of the law. But such plausibility and authority is deceptive. The exact meaning of any right that is claimed, and whether the right claimed is justified, must be clarified in further debate. The language of rights, because of its con-clusive, peremptory nature, does not invite any discussion, even though further discussion is necessary. What language is available then for the further debate? There cannot be a recourse to law for a decision, because the point at issue is precisely the question of what the law should be. Nor can it be a matter of asserting some moral right as requiring immediate incorporation in positive law, since that presupposes that the very debate which is required has already taken place. I wish to argue that the debate on such issues ultimately relies on some understanding of the human good which informs the articulation of moral rights, which then may or may not be incorporated in positive law. The disagreements which first appear as a conflict of rights asserted on the moral level are in reality rooted in differing conceptions of and commitments to the human good. One cannot completely avoid engaging in some discussion between competing and incompatible comprehensive doctrines, because it is frequently the case that the terms relied upon in the political debate derive their meaning from the broader background.

THE HUMAN GOOD

The understanding of what constitutes the human good is fundamental for specifying the content of moral rights and duties. This is well illustrated in the case of the asserted 'right to control what happens in and to one's body'. What precisely is meant by this right is unclear. Does it include the right to suicide, to self-mutilation, to the unhindered abuse of alcohol or other drugs? These are instances of 'control over what happens in and to one's body'. Normally this right is meaning-fully asserted in areas where bodily integrity and personal autonomy are in danger of being violated by others, for example in cases of rape or medical experimentation without consent. The assertion of a person's autonomy is what is central. Intimacy forced on a non-consenting person is a fundamental violation, depriving that person of the autonomous control of her activity. To perform operations on patients without their consent, or to undertake medical experimentation without prior agreement, is to deny people the control over their own destiny which rightfully should be theirs.

These assertions of what should be are derived from a vision of what is good, namely personal autonomy and the exercise of responsibility in one's own destiny. Such cases as those presented above provide the core meaning for the asserted right to control what happens in and to one's body. But if the meaning of the asserted right to control over one's body is specified in terms of such cases as sexual violation and unpermitted medical experimentation, it is clear that the meaning of the right cannot be extended without further argument to include a right to self-mutilation or destruction. And *a fortiori*, it cannot include a right to harm another. The meaning of asserted moral rights is rooted in some understanding of the human good which in turn must be presented and defended in a language other than that of rights.

THE RIGHT TO WORK

The difficulties with the language of rights can be illustrated from the case of the frequently claimed right to work. In the context of growing unemployment the plight of those without work is often formulated in terms of this right: they are said to be denied their right to work. The assertion of this right to work is not only to be found in political positions on the left: it is also expressly made in Catholic social teaching. For instance, the 1986 *Instruction on Christian Freedom and Liberation* states that 'every person has a right to work, and this right must be recognised in a practical way by an effective commitment to resolving the tragic problem of unemployment'.[3] This assertion is rooted in an understanding of the dignity of work and of its importance for the human person. To be denied the opportunity of working and contributing to the productive efforts of society is to be restricted in one's humanity. This is because work and creative activity are considered integral to what it means to be human. Typically, such explanations of the meaning of this right appeal to the notion of participation and argue that if one is denied the opportunity of participating in one's society in one of the ways valued in that society, then one is deprived of something essential to human dignity.

Such explanations attempt to justify the asserted moral right by reflecting on values rooted in a particular vision of the human good: participation, creative investment of productive energies, fulfilment in the actualisation of specifically human capacities, and such like. When speaking of the human good in this manner it is entirely plausible to say that all share a responsibility for ensuring that the human dignity of each is respected. So for instance the document quoted above goes on to say that 'the creation of jobs is a primary social task facing individuals and private enterprise as well as the state'.[4] Other expressions of this vision rely on the notion of 'solidarity', whereby 'all are really responsible for all'.[5]

This vision of the human good and of the responsibility of all is appealed to in making sense of the assertion that there is a right to work. And yet, when the assertion is transposed into a more technical idiom of rights, the meaning of the assertion becomes problematic, because rights by definition are either liberties or claim-rights, and the assertion of a right to work obliges one to say whether the right asserted is a liberty or a claim.[6]

LIBERTIES AND CLAIM-RIGHTS

A person is said to have a right in the sense of liberty in relation to some action or good if she is not bound by some relevant duty. So for instance John is at liberty to travel to Dublin if he is not prevented by some relevant duty from doing so. His obligations to respect the property of transport companies and abide by the regulations, or to spend his time working in fulfilment of existing contracts, could be relevant duties. On the other hand, one is said to have a claim-right to some action or good if there is some other person who has a corresponding duty. So for instance Mary could be said to have a claim-right to a ticket to Dublin because the travel agent has a duty to provide her with one. This duty could be derived from a contract of sale. The assertion of a claim-right to some good always presupposes the identification of an individual person who is bound by duty to provide some good or perform some action. This distinction between liberties and claim-rights applies to both legal and moral rights.

In the strict language of rights, only identifiable individuals or legal persons can be considered to have duties corresponding to claim-rights. It is meaningless within this framework to ascribe a duty or duties to 'all', to the 'whole society' or to the 'system'. Only individuals can be thought to have duties corresponding to others' rights. But there are no identifiable individuals in this sense who have a duty to employ the unemployed. If there were, the problem would be much simpler. It would be simply a matter of saying Guinness should employ so many, Smith's should employ so many, Cadbury's so many, and so on, and then it would be clear who is and who is not fulfilling their duty. Since it is impossible to identify such individuals as bound by duties, it is meaningless within this framework to say that the unemployed have a claim-right to work.

The origin of rights language in legal discourse is evident in these definitions. However, the legal discourse in question reflects the liberal agenda of protecting individual liberty against the arbitrary exercise of power. The individualism permeating this dominant liberal model of rights imposes a restriction on what can be said in the language of rights. As a result the assertion of a right to work is reduced to a slogan, and cannot function as an argument in the strict sense.[7] To make it effective the vision of the human good behind this assertion must be presented for discussion in a language which is free from such restrictions.

In debates about what rights ought to be secured and enforced in law, reliance on the present language of moral rights is unhelpful for two reasons. First, because the meaning of the rights asserted must be established by resorting to a further level of debate, and second, because the language of rights as shaped by the dominant legal framework imposes restrictions which limit what can be said in this language.

THE RELATION OF MORAL TO LEGAL RIGHTS

My argument has been that the meaning of moral rights needs to be clarified by debate at the level of the human good. The relationship between these two levels presents one tension in this difficult arena of political conflict. But there is also the further tension between the levels of moral and legal rights. Are all moral rights to be incorporated in legal rights? And are legal rights to be deduced from moral rights as their only source? This tension reflects a complexity in the understanding of the human good.

PROSTITUTION

I lived in a city for a number of years in which my legal right to the services of a prostitute was secured. Since prostitution was permitted under licence, I was at liberty in law to avail of the relevant services. I had a right to them, in the sense of liberty. But of course it does not follow from the existence of a legal right that there is a corresponding moral right. Prostitution was permitted under licence for a number of reasons related to public order rather than to the unrestricted human good. Prostitution was tolerated, firstly, in order to maintain some control over what the legislators recognised was going to happen anyway, secondly, to minimise the ancillary crimes commonly associated with prostitution and the abuse of the persons involved by pimps and others which criminalising prostitution would facilitate, and thirdly, with a view to public health, to maintain control over sexually transmitted diseases by requiring regular health checks. These are reasons why rights might be accorded by positive law, which do not include any moral approbation of prostitution.

SUICIDE

In Britain there is a right to suicide. This is a legal right secured in law, since the UK 1961 Suicide Act decriminalised suicide.[8] The law was changed, not because parliament wished to propagate the view that suicide was a good option which people ought to consider, but because the legislators were agreed that punishment for a crime was an inadequate response by society to people who had failed in their suicide attempts. Some response other than punishment was seen to be desirable. And so removing attempted suicide from the list of crimes had the effect of legally permitting suicide, not that some supposed moral right to suicide might be incorporated in law, but so that some adequate response to the social phenomenon of suicide might be made possible.

However, on the basis of the existing legal right to suicide, the Voluntary Euthanasia Society (VES) argues that this right acknowledges a moral right to suicide. To be meaningful, the society argues further, such a moral right to suicide would have to be linked to a moral right to be helped kill oneself, since many of those who would wish to commit suicide do not have the physical strength or the means at their disposal; on the basis of these asserted moral rights, the VES demands that legal rights to voluntary euthanasia be secured in law.[9]

Leaving aside the failure to distinguish between rights as liberty (to suicide) and claim-rights (to be helped to kill oneself), let us focus on the question of the relation between moral rights and legal rights. Does it follow from the fact of a legal right that there is a moral right, as the VES argument supposes? And does it follow from the conviction of a moral right that there should be a legal right? It is clear from the intentions of the legislators in introducing the Suicide Act 1961 that they did not wish morally to condone suicide; on the contrary, they explicitly maintained stiff penalties for those who would act to assist suicides. Their main concern was to establish a more appropriate response by society to failed suicides. In order to establish the moral duties and rights and wrongs in relation to suicide, it would be necessary to explore this issue in terms of the human good: what constitutes the good for a person, and what is the good to be striven for and protected in the face of death and prolonged suffering? Such questions must be handled on their own merits. There are no short-cuts by means of peremptory assertions of moral rights.

PUBLIC ORDER

The considerations involved in deciding which moral rights ought to be included in the positive list of legal rights, and which legal rights should be secured, cannot be drawn from the debate on the level of the human good alone. These must also include considerations of what is conducive to public order and the common good. Is it the same to say 'there ought to be a legal right', and 'there is a moral right'? On the face of it, the use of the word 'ought' seems to suggest a moral basis to the demand for the creation of a legal right. But the cases of suicide and prostitution discussed above illustrate how it can be reasonable to enact legal rights for reasons other than the moral status of the relevant activities. Such reasons have to do with public order, the balance of advantages and disadvantages with regard to the ordering of social life. The considerations of control, crime levels and public health in the case of prostitution illustrate this type of reasoning. The enactment of legal rights on such grounds does not imply any moral approbation of the relevant activities. But of course, one of the disadvantages to be weighed in the balance is the fact that some people will understand the existence of a legal right as evidence of a moral right. We can see this happening in the VES reading of the 'right to suicide'.

CONCLUSION

The argument of this chapter can be summarised in the following points. Much political debate about what the law should be relies on a distinction between moral rights and legal rights. Moral rights are often asserted in the context of debates about what legal rights ought to be secured in positive law. There is frequently a presupposition in such debates that there is some automatic deduction from moral to legal rights. I deny the validity of such a presupposition. Moral rights are often asserted as if their meaning and ground of justification were self-evident. I argue that the meaning of moral rights can be established only against the background of a description or theory of the human good. The two-tier model of moral and legal rights must be expanded to include a third tier appropriate to the horizon of debate about the human good. It is not possible to indicate the content of any right independently of any consideration of the good which is at stake. Examples of this are asserted rights to control over what happens in and to one's body, asserted rights to property, asserted rights to suicide and euthanasia. This first point has to do with the meaning of moral rights. A further point has to do with the relation between moral and legal rights. I have argued that there is no automatic connection between moral rights and legal rights. In order to determine what the legal rights ought to be in any community, appeal to the level of moral rights can be only one aspect of the process. Those moral rights are to be understood in the light of some reflection on the human good. However, the determination of what the legal rights ought to be will depend on a reflection on public order. Considerations of public order may often lead to situations in which what is morally wrong may be legally permitted, that is, where legal rights are secured to goods or actions to which there are no moral rights. Examples are suicide in UK law, and prostitution in Austria. Distinguishing between moral and legal rights in public debate is often therefore difficult and requires a high degree of sophistication. Education for citizenship in liberal democracies in which concern for human rights characterises public debate must include education for literacy for such debate. To recognise this and to undertake the necessary steps in promoting an appropriate education and a defence of the liberal regime mean that one must move beyond a merely neutral stance in relation to the state and its institutions. The problems which this raises for a liberal philosopher will be addressed in the next chapter.

CHAPTER 7

THE DEBATE ON THE HUMAN GOOD

My principal topic in the last three chapters has been the notion of public order. This was introduced in Chapter 4 to identify that restricted domain of the common good which is the appropriate focus of politics and the state. I conceded to MacIntyre that the modern state could not be the moral educator which Aristotle expected the *polis* to be, nor could it be the forum for achieving the good life for humans in the unrestricted sense. Augustine's reflections had also been valuable in making this distinction. The notion of public order was useful for outlining a common good of cooperation in the political sphere. In Chapter 5 I surveyed a number of ways in which liberal philosophers typically specify public order, namely, as the guarantee of law and order, as the protection of liberty, and as neutrality between competing views of the human good. I argued that these minimalist specifications of public order were too restricted and that there are valid concerns which would allow us to give a broader content to the notion. In the last chapter I continued the discussion of public order by illustrating its role in the creation and specification of legal rights, the usual focus of public debate, especially involving issues of law and morality. In this chapter I want to continue the discussion of public order and specifically to investigate whether it is confined to the realm of means or if it overlaps with some of the ends which make up the unrestricted human good.

Especially in the context of wanting to maintain neutrality

116

between competing visions of the human good, liberal thinkers have argued that they are not directly concerned with any of the ends which belong to the various versions of the human good. Rather, they have claimed that their focus has been the provision of means which are neutral between the competing versions of ends. So, for instance, the free market does not favour one competitor over another, the protection of liberty gives no advantage to any one person's projects and the protection of freedom of speech does not discriminate between objectives. These are some of the means typically advocated by liberal positions. As noted in Chapter 5 and in a different context in Chapter 6, the liberal agenda developed in reaction against the tyranny of autocratic and arbitrary rule. It sought recognition and respect for the autonomy and freedom of individuals in contexts in which these were violated.[1] The claim of neutrality was consistent with this advocacy stance. But now the situation is different. There are states which understand themselves as embodying liberal ideals and principles. The intellectual task of the liberal thinker is different in this context. Now the liberal is engaged in legitimating actual political systems and in providing a defence for structures and policy in those systems. Neutrality between competing positions on the ends of human life may still be a liberal value, but the liberal thinker is not necessarily neutral in relation to the state. He is now committed to advocating and promoting certain features of the legal and political system operative in his liberal society. As MacIntyre puts it:

> Liberalism thus provides a distinctive conception of a just order which is closely integrated with the conception of practical reasoning required by public transactions conducted within the terms set by a liberal polity. The principles which inform such practical reasoning and the theory and practice of justice within such a polity are not neutral with respect to rival and conflicting theories of the human good. Where they are in force they impose a particular conception of the good life, of practical reasoning and of justice upon those who willingly or unwillingly accept the liberal procedures and the liberal terms of debate. The overriding good of liberalism is no more and no less than the continued sustenance of the liberal social and political order.[2]

Many liberal thinkers recognise that there is a new situation and that they have to reconsider their position in relation to the good.[3] They are being forced to do so by problems arising within liberal political systems. One such problem is the need for governments to decide on a trade-off between equality and liberty. Commitment to diminishing inequalities through affirmative action programmes or redistributive taxation is at the expense of some whose liberties are curtailed. Which is the liberal policy as such? There is no one liberal position; rather, liberal philosophies divide on the issue and generate alternative schools of thought, whether libertarian liberalism or egalitarian liberalism, or whatever. In liberal democracies the political problems are concrete and real; the theoretical positions do not have the luxury of simply criticising a system which is rejected in principle, but inevitably must provide some measure of legitimacy for one or other political stance. The liberal does not remain neutral but takes a stand in favour of some good.

RAWLS'S THIN THEORY OF THE GOOD

It is possible to trace this problem in the writings of a contemporary exponent of the liberal position, John Rawls. Rawls is frequently characterised as an egalitarian liberal, in contrast to the libertarian liberalism of Robert Nozick, for instance. Here the contrast is in terms of the trade-off between equality and liberty. While this classification is not entirely satisfactory, it does point to a concern about inequality which marked out Rawls's work in contrast to other liberal positions. While his ideas were unmistakeably liberal in giving priority to liberty, he attempted to integrate a concern for economic, social and political equality in his essentially liberal theory.

However, Rawls is a traditional liberal in the sense of preserving neutrality on the question of the good. Assuming that people could not be expected to agree on the ultimate goals of their lives, or on the content of the conception of the good life, he focused on the range of goods which he thought anyone would want to have as means to their goals. Whatever they want to pursue in life, it can be assumed that people will want the liberties necessary to framing and pursuing their individual ends and they will want to have the financial and material resources to enable them to get what they want. Rawls lists these general means under the heading of primary goods:

(a) basic rights and liberties, also given by a list
(b) freedom of movement and free choice of occupation against a background of diverse opportunities
(c) powers and prerogatives of offices and positions of responsibility in the political and economic institutions of the basic structure
(d) income and wealth
(e) the social bases of self-respect.[4]

Because these are means, Rawls considers that people would want them for the sake of their goals, whatever their goals might turn out to be. As such they are presumed to be neutral between different conceptions of a life-plan and between different conceptions of justice.

These primary social goods play a significant part in the construction of the two principles of justice which comprise the core of the account of justice in Rawls's *A Theory of Justice*. The first principle advocates the allocation to each citizen of as great a range of liberties as is consistent with the liberties of others; the second principle regulates the distribution of the other goods but will only tolerate inequalities in their distribution on two conditions, namely, that the existence of inequalities results in improving the position of the worst-off in the society, and the inequalities are attached to positions which are open to all in a context of equal opportunity. Rawls also indicates a priority in the ordering of these two principles: the first must be satisfied in full before the second is applicable, so that there is no trade-off allowed between liberty and equality.[5]

Rawls's argument in favour of these two principles is that they would be chosen by rational agents who were required to choose principles to regulate their social life while being ignorant of their own place in the society and even of their own life-plans and ultimate goals. This ignorance ensures that they are freed from the distorting influence of their personal interests or those of their family or social group. Behind this 'veil of ignorance', knowing only that they would want to have as much of the primary social goods as possible, Rawls argues that rational choosers would choose his principles in preference to all others. So in generating his theory of justice Rawls does rely on a theory of the good, but he can qualify it as a 'thin' theory which does not commit him to any substantive account of the good. Where a 'thick' theory would elaborate the content of a vision of the goals of human life, Rawls is content that his 'thin' theory remains neutral over against the range of such visions, since it only covers goods which are means to any life-plan. However, critical reactions to this theory suggested that he was in danger of attempting a comprehensive moral theory and a complete social philosophy. This is because he seemed to be providing a comprehensive account of what would be a rational justification in practical matters.

These criticisms led him to refine the presentation of his ideas in a series of essays which were later collected in a second book, *Political Liberalism.* The main point of the later book is that the theory Rawls is attempting to offer is to be considered a political as distinct from a comprehensive moral theory. His ideas articulate the nature of a political system which could count on the rational agreement of citizens who otherwise disagree with one another on philosophical and moral and religious matters. Thus he could imagine people of differing religious allegiance and of none cooperating in the maintenance of his political system; also people who might otherwise hold heated arguments with one another about moral matters, Aristotelians, Kantians and utilitarians for instance, could be expected to agree on political liberalism. And this is the sense in which Rawls considers his view of liberalism a political as distinct from a comprehensive doctrine. It is offered for a situation in which a plurality of comprehensive moral and religious doctrines compete with one another, but can count on the rational support of adherents of all the doctrines, without favouring any one of them.

In his earlier work *A Theory of Justice* Rawls seems to be relying on a combination of two distinctions which are separated in the later book *Political Liberalism.* One is the distinction between means and ends; the second is the distinction between a thin theory of the good and a thick theory. The means–goal distinction is unproblematic. The other distinction is drawn betweeen what is capable of agreement between conflicting parties and what is incapable of such agreement. The combination of these two and their application to the primary social goods suggests that agreement in a conflict situation could only be expected with regard to means and not ends, and that a thin theory of the good will be a theory of means. The separation of these two distinctions allows for the recognition that a thin account of the good, one capable of receiving rational support from participants, could include some ends. And so, for instance, he acknowledges in the later work that the system of political justice in a situation of rational pluralism is not itself simply a means to the realisation of individuals' life-plans. He admits that citizens in a well-ordered society do have at least one final end in common, namely, 'the end of supporting just institutions and of giving one another justice accordingly, not to mention many other ends they must also share and realise through their political arrangements'.[6] Therefore the relationship of the political good of a well-ordered society to the ultimate goods identified in comprehensive religious, philosophical or moral doctrine is not that of means to ends. Rather, he seems to envisage a great range of final ends, but some of these qualify as belonging to a political conception because they attain the rational support of adherents of conflicting comprehensive doctrines, and they identify what is required for harmonious social existence in the context of a plurality of rational comprehensive doctrines. Rawls's theory continues to be 'thin', but not in the sense that the 'thinness' involves restriction to means.

This development was necessary because of criticisms levelled at the early work. It was queried whether the primary social goods were really neutral between different life-plans, or if they did not favour particular, historically conditioned views of the good life. It was pointed out that even the specification of the primary goods was such that it presupposed a whole history of development of political and economic life, and a valuing of liberties, powers and opportunities which was itself rooted in a history. The supposedly neutral primary goods seemed laden with an option for a particular kind of society and a particular kind of political existence, namely, the liberal democracy exemplified in North America. Rawls adjusted to this criticism by acknowledging that the kind of society he is envisaging is a definite good which has its historical and economic conditions.

THICK, VAGUE THEORY

This development in Rawls's thought illustrates in its own way the point I am making about the reawakening of the question of the good in liberal thought. However, Rawls's coining of the phrase 'thin theory of the good' provides a useful foil for an Aristotelian scholar who has recently attempted to contribute to this development within liberalism from an Aristotelian perspective.[7] Philosophers in the Aristotelian tradition are always interested in the question of the human good but in the context of contemporary debate they have to bear in mind the concerns of those who are protective of liberty. The challenge for the Aristotelian therefore is to articulate a vision of the good life which allows proper scope for individual liberty, and which does not constitute a threat to autonomy. Martha Nussbaum attempts to do this. She acknowledges that a 'thick' theory of the good which articulates the content of a comprehensive doctrine of human ends is unacceptable in the context of a modern liberal society. It is also likely to favour the purposes of some groups over others. On the other hand, purely thin versions of the good are insufficient to motivate support for the maintenance and administration of institutions for the protection of liberty. Her proposal is a 'thick, vague conception of the good'.[8] She offers a thick conception in that she lists people's purposes and ends in a range of areas of life, but in such a way that the formulation of the ends is vague, allowing for a rich variety of specifications. For instance, our bodiliness, and its associated need for food and drink, finds expression in the many cultures with their different cuisines. Nussbaum is aware of the misgivings of many philosophers that ideas with an Aristotelian heritage are usually linked to ideas about a universal human nature which would downplay the myriad varieties of human culture. She avoids this suspicion by drawing on the story-telling and myth-making imagination rather than the scientific intellect in identifying the characteristics of being human. She offers a list of characteristics which are based on the commonness of myths and stories from many times and places, stories explaining to both friends and strangers what it is to be human. Such stories allow people to recognise humanness at a distance, and as such they express the answer to questions like: 'What are the features of our common humanity, features that lead us to recognise certain others, however distant their location and their forms of life, as humans?'[9] She insists that the list of features is open-ended and not systematic; it is not intended as a definition, but to direct attention to certain areas of special importance.

The list identifies both limits and capacities which characterise the human condition: mortality; bodiliness: hunger and thirst, need for shelter, sexual desire; mobility; capacity for pleasure and pain; cognitive capability: perceiving, imagining, thinking; early infant development; practical reason; affiliation with other human beings; relatedness to other species and to nature; humour and play; separateness; strong separateness. True to her Aristotelian sources Nussbaum emphasises people's capabilities for functioning in the tension between these limits and capacities. In relation to each of the items on her list she formulates human functional capabilities, such as

> being able to use the five senses; to imagine to think and reason; being able to have attachments to things and persons outside ourselves, to those who love and care for us, to grieve at their absence, to love, to grieve, to feel longing and gratitude; being able to form a conception of the good and to engage in critical reflection about the planning of one's own life; being able to live for and to others, to recognise and show concern for other human

beings, to engage in various forms of familial and social interaction.[10]

Her claim is that a life lacking any of these capabilities will be
seriously lacking in humanness. Of the functionings listed,
two are particularly significant, namely, practical reasoning
and affiliation with others. These are architectonic in that they
will be operative in all the functionings, which are planned by
practical reason and done with and to others.[11]

The task of politics is specified in terms of this view of the
human good. The focus is not so much on ensuring that people
in fact flourish and function well in all respects, but rather on
ensuring that all citizens have the personal resources so that
they have the capability of functioning well. So the political
system commensurate with a thick, vague conception of the
good would be designed to ensure that citizens receive the
institutional, material and educational support that is required
if they are to become capable of functioning well in each
sphere according to their own practical reason. Insofar as the
state system is to provide welfare to its citizens, the understanding of welfare is not residual, picking up those who have
fallen through various nets and have not been able to fend
for themselves. Rather, it is institutional, aimed at facilitating
all citizens by means of a comprehensive support scheme of
health care and education for their functioning in a range of
areas over a complete life. Treating citizens as free and equal
means moving all of them across a threshold into capability to
choose well, should the available resources permit this.
Nussbaum sketches the sort of protection of liberties and rights
which would be required in order to ensure the qualities of
separateness and autonomy valued by this thick conception
of the human good. And so on the question whether there
will not inevitably be tension between the value of well-being
and the value of individual choice she is confident that her
proposal includes a sufficiently strong protection for liberty.
Her response is not simply defensive: she challenges an
excessively abstracted idea of liberty and choice in order to
highlight the conditions of exercising freedom. The capability

to choose good functioning within each sphere and the capability of choosing at all, quite generally, have complex social and material necessary conditions, conditions not likely to exist without strong government intervention. The liberal state may content itself with a purely negative defence of liberty; the Aristotelian social democratic state would be committed to sustaining the conditions which enable all its citizens to function as autonomous beings.

Nussbaum asks whether the liberal regard for a pluralist society, and respect for the equality of citizens as choosers of their own conceptions of the good, are compatible with her thick conception of the good. She acknowledges the liberal suspicion of an Aristotelian view. It is suspected of opting for a single conception of good rather than a plurality, and that in the process it tells people what they should be, asking them to live the life that a supremely wise man thinks would be best for them. This removes their moral autonomy, and treats them unequally. But she argues that her conception of the good, while thick, is vague, and is designed to admit of plural specifications. This she thinks saves it from the usual criticisms.

CONCLUSION

Nussbaum's exploration provides a good example of the kind of discussion argued for in the previous chapter. Whatever about the determination of legal rights, the assertion of human or moral rights requires a context within which they can be understood. Our political culture needs a forum in which the question of the human good can be addressed. Nussbaum offers one proposal to meet this need, in her thick vague conception of the human good. This is a useful and interesting proposal, and while I find it attractive, I am not advocating it here. Rather it serves as an example for the kind of discussion which I consider necessary, a discussion which may never be conclusive. It is a discussion aimed at articulating the common good of political community. In this case, the good which is commonly recognised is the flourishing and good functioning of any human being.[12] What is expressed by the emphasis on the vagueness of the description of that good is the recognition that people must be allowed scope to determine for themselves how precisely they will realise the various aspects of their vaguely described good. Therefore it cannot be the concern of government to decide people's good for them, or to make them good. However, government does need some conception of what constitutes good human functioning in order to create and sustain the appropriate conditions which enable people to identify and pursue their own good. It is also worth noting the emphasis which Nussbaum places on myth and story. The exploration of the human good can rely on narrative and especially on the stories of lives available to us from biography and autobiography. It is a matter of developing possibly shared ideas of a life worth living, not in order that political authority might force people to conform to some selected pattern of a life, but so that the political community would facilitate people's achievement of their good through the provision of relevant conditions. These conditions are not universal, neutral means, and they cannot be identified without consideration of the ends. Hence the need for the public space in which issues of the human good can be explored. The review of the development in Rawls's thought confirms this conclusion. His clarification of his ideas has also removed the suspicion that the common good of public order is merely a means, neutral between competing ends. It can be seen to some extent as part of the ends of citizens who value the liberty and the quality of social life which is made possible in a liberal polity. The purposes of the liberal state are genuine common goods, even if restricted.

CHAPTER 8

SECURING A PUBLIC SPACE

My argument in favour of a language broad enough to encompass the full range of human cooperation has been extended into an argument about the need for a forum for public debate. Reliance on models of rationality which are based on self-interest imposes restrictions on what can be argued. But similarly, the assumption that the political forum is an arena in which conflicting parties, fundamentally divided on the question of the good, meet to negotiate some accommodation, imposes restrictions on what may be discussed. It is frequently assumed that the issues of the good are excluded from the agenda. In liberal accounts, this exclusion is usually argued for on the basis that agreement on the good is not achievable since there are no rational grounds for personal preferences. In my argument I have tried to show the traps into which we can be led by this Humean psychology (Chapter 2). But also I have argued positively that another reading of the liberal position requires some discussion at least of the human good. Two instances were particularly important. In the context of the discussion of Mill's liberty principle I argued that his provision that society might be warranted in limiting liberties to prevent harm to itself would require discussion of the social interests at stake (Chapter 5). And where political debate relies on the language of rights I suggested there is need for discussion of the human good in order to establish the meaning and range of rights claimed (Chapter 6).

Two further suggestions clarify what is being proposed. The first and more important is the distinction between the common good and public order (Chapter 4). The notion of public order allowed a restriction of the agenda to those aspects of the good which are accessible to political action. The second was a suggestion that the use of a 'thick, vague conception of the good' would allow a discussion of the human good to the extent that it was needed for the purposes of social existence, without requiring participants in the debate to subscribe to a definite position on the ultimate human good (Chapter 7). These are clarifications of the agenda, and also of the language available for the debate. But I am suggesting also that this debate on the human good requires its own forum, at some remove from the heated atmosphere of politics in the narrow sense. And for a vibrant political culture it is not sufficient that the debate be conducted solely by academics or in the university setting exclusively. Perhaps the notion of civil society is appropriate here: a buffer between the individual citizen and the state, a forum in which individuals and groups can engage in debate without their disagreements being translated immediately into political options. Such a forum would itself be part of the conditions for the good of public order. Love of liberty would require maintenance of such a forum in which liberty in Mill's sense could be fostered.

There is a question which must be faced, however. In the Introduction I asked whether the language of the common good can be part of the overlapping consensus in a liberal and pluralist society. I have been arguing that it can be, but I also must be realistic and acknowledge that there are many for whom any rhetoric of the common good is a threat to liberty. For those who see the notion of the common good as a sectarian notion, the qualifications developed above in terms of public order and a thick, vague conception of the good will not allay their suspicions. Their fear is that arguments in terms of the common good and appeals for a forum for public debate are merely a cover-up for attempts to acquire the backing of coercive political power for a particular substantive position on the good. It would be unrealistic of me to discuss these issues in an Irish context without adverting to the fact that in Ireland the Catholic Church's use of the language of the common good is made the target of similar suspicions. It is often suggested that those who present the Catholic position are attempting to impose on the state and society views which are only intelligible on the presupposition of religious faith. To the extent that the Catholic Church's position relies on an understanding of the common good, it is important for me to consider this charge if I am to sustain my argument that the language of the common good is both necessary and useful for a liberal political culture.

In the last twenty years Ireland has seen a series of debates on matters of law and morality. All who have participated know exactly how heated the debate can become. Emotions frequently run high because the issues at stake typically touch on people's fundamental religious and moral convictions as well as on their own personal experience of pain and suffering. The many issues which have provoked this heated debate have been about law, both criminal and constitutional. Debated changes to the criminal law included decriminalising homosexual activity and legalising the sale of contraceptives, while the controversial changes to the constitution included the addition of protection for unborn life and the removal of the ban on divorce law. These have been debates about the law, but what has made them particularly heated has been the connection with moral issues. People are not used to having their moral standards called into question in debate; these standards they accept as the basis from which to consider concrete problems or particularly difficult issues. But in a debate on what the law should be, people must be capable of calling into question whether the law need be or should be as it has been received. They must be capable of a flexibility in relation to the law which one would not expect of them in relation to their own moral standards. Such a capacity would presuppose an ability to distinguish in practice between law and morality. Debates on the law therefore require a space all of their own, removed from the distinctively moral. Granted that the Catholic Church has its own highly developed perspective on morality, does it also have a position on the function of law in a secular society which is sufficiently removed from and independent of its moral teaching? Is its view in relation to law capable of representation in an overlapping consensus?

The public debates on law and morality, as well as the New Ireland Forum, have given the Irish Catholic bishops the opportunity to clarify publicly their position in regard to the law. The series of statements which they produced contain both a negative and a positive message. The negative message is the denial of any direct connection between the moral teaching and what the law ought to be: 'We do not ask that Catholic doctrine as such be enshrined in law'.[1] How well individual churchmen have adhered in practice to this separation is another question; my concern here is to consider the position as articulated. There is evidence within the published statements of a developing commitment by the bishops to a distinction between the spheres of morality and of law. This development is the product of a learning process stimulated by the shift in approach taken by the Second Vatican Council in its discussion of the grounds for religious liberty. The council, in its *Declaration on Religious Liberty*, insisted that 'all should be immune from coercion on the part of individuals, social groups and every human power, so that, within due limits, nobody is forced to act against his convictions nor is anyone to be restrained from acting in accordance with his convictions in religious matters in private or in public, alone or in association with others'.[2] Patrick Hannon in his book *Church, State, Morality and Law* argues that this principle, which was articulated for the right to religious liberty, becomes a guiding principle for other aspects of social life.[3] In other words, just as the state through its laws should not attempt to coerce people, positively or negatively, in matters of religious belief and practice, so also should it not attempt to restrict or coerce people in matters which affect their freedom of action in accordance with their own conscience. Does this imply that people should never be restricted by state law from exercising their freedom? The council does not go so far. There is a qualification, hinted at above in the quoted phrase 'within due limits'. The exercise of freedom should not be hindered, according to paragraph 7 of the same declaration, except when and in so far as is necessary for 'the just requirements of public order', of peace, justice and public morality. But what is required for the maintenance of public order and justice is not immediately evident. It is precisely here that we find the space for debate arising out of legitimate disagreement. Politicians and voters are faced with the challenge of forming an opinion on what is best conducive to public order, and on the limits to be imposed on individuals' liberties for the sake of that common good.

Acknowledgement of the separation of law from morality is the negative aspect of the church's message, denying any direct relevance of its moral teaching for the making of civil law. The positive aspect is the highlighting of responsibility for the just requirements of public order as the relevant consideration for formulating the content of civil law. The double message is that in matters of law and morality those with the responsibility of making the law must ask, not so much: 'what is moral?', or 'what is the church's teaching?', but: 'what is best for public order and public morality?' And because the conditions needed for public order are the subject of debate and disagreement between concerned citizens, this positive aspect of the position amounts to the insistence that there be another space, a separate forum, for debates about the law, even when they concern moral matters. The church's advocacy for responsibility for the common good, as formulated in its published statements, is consistent with the respect for individual liberty and the protection of a forum for unconstrained public debate as appropriate to an overlapping consensus in a liberal pluralist society.

LEARNING FROM MILL AND AQUINAS

I suggest that this development can be seen as the learning of the Catholic Church about politics. This has been a slow adjustment to the Enlightenment themes of liberty and rights, which were regarded suspiciously by the church, not least because of the extreme anti-clericalism of many of their proponents. But while it has taken the church a long time to adjust to the situation of liberal democracy in the Northern and Western world, its learning has been as much a recovery of elements of its own heritage as a discovery of new realities. The Vatican Council's statements echo John Stuart Mill's championing of liberty, but they are also consistent with the ideas of Thomas Aquinas on the relationship between the state's law and the moral law. Aquinas asked whether human law should prohibit all wrongdoing, or command acts of all the virtues. In his discussion of these questions, it is clear that he did not envisage a direct inference from the moral to the legal. Whether or not some activity, known to be immoral, should be prohibited in the civil law, depends on the impact that activity has on society. Aquinas points out that certain actions like murder and theft could not be tolerated, not because of their wrongfulness, but because they would make social existence impossible:

> . . . human laws do not forbid all vices from which the virtuous abstain but only the more grievous vices from which it is possible for the majority to abstain and chiefly those that are to the hurt of others, without the prohibition of which human society could not be maintained; thus human law prohibits murder, theft, and suchlike.[4]

Worthy of note in Aquinas's formulation is the reference to the possibility of hurt to others which would be a reason for proscribing certain activities. Unless one feels secure in the knowledge that one's life and possession of things which are important for the maintenance of life will not be violated, one would be very reluctant to engage in interaction with others. And so in order to facilitate the kind of interaction which is essential for society, civil law would prohibit murder and theft. The reasons for prohibiting certain actions are formulated in terms of impact on society rather than the moral status of those actions. Similarly, when it comes to the actions which the law should command, Aquinas considers that the law would explicitly command only those activities which are necessary

for the common good of the society, which he in this context
identifies as the requirements of justice and peace:

> ... human law does not prescribe concerning all the acts of every
> virtue but only in regard to those that are ordained to the common
> good – either immediately, as when certain things are done directly
> for the common good, or mediately, as when a lawgiver prescribes
> certain things pertaining to good training whereby the citizens
> are disciplined in the upholding of the common good of justice
> and peace.[5]

In this treatment of the relationship between law and
morality Aquinas is applying insights learned from Augustine,
and combining them with his Aristotelian heritage. This
combination is not an immediately obvious one; on the
contrary, it would seem that Aristotle and Augustine have
radically opposed views on the nature of civil law. Aristotle is
explicit in affirming that the objective of lawmakers in making
law is to make citizens good. Law should be part of the moral
education of citizens which would fit them to participate in
the good life which is the point of politics. Augustine on the
other hand rejected the idea that human institutions as such
could make people good. All that he could expect from civil
law is that it would apply coercive means to control the socially
destructive forces at work in human hearts. And as discussed
in Chapter 4 above, Augustine suspected the law and its officers
of being imbued with the same destructiveness as they are
intended to control. Aquinas manages to combine the insights
of his two authorities, accepting both that the law's purpose is
to make people good, and that the law is an instrument of
control for the purposes of social peace. This he does by
qualifying the goodness which is the proper object of human
law. Agreeing with Augustine he recognises that the goodness
of citizens which can be achieved by means of human law is
not their ultimate good, but is nonetheless a genuine good.
This distinction is evident in his discussion of the effects of
law. He admits that law makes its subjects good, but he
distinguishes the meaning of good: 'the proper effect of law is
to make those to whom it is given good, either simply or in

some particular respect'.[6] In response to an objection he
clarifies what might be the particular respects in which citizens
are to be good. It is clear that it might be sufficient for a citizen
to be deemed good that she abide by the law. 'The common
good of the political community cannot flourish unless the
citizens be virtuous, at least those whose business it is to govern.
But it is enough for the good of the community that the other
citizens be so far virtuous that they obey the commands of
their rulers.'[7] It is quite acceptable to Aquinas that this be
achieved by means of the coercive force of the civil law, even if
there are many citizens who can be law abiding without the
threat of punishment. For them the directive force of the law
is what guides their actions.

> Since some are found to be depraved and prone to vice and not
> easily amenable to words, it was necessary for such to be restrained
> from evil by force and fear in order that they might at least desist
> from evil-doing and leave others in peace, and that they
> themselves, by being habituated in this way, might be brought to
> do willingly what hitherto they did from fear and thus become
> virtuous. Now this kind of training which compels through fear
> of punishment is the discipline of laws.[8]

Here again is that very contemporary-sounding reference to
restraining some so as to leave others in peace.

Aquinas's position leads to practical implications for the
civil law, very similar to those deriving from J. S. Mill's principle.
And yet the similar practical implications derive from different
concerns. Aquinas is concerned with what is necessary for
society to exist and survive, and what is necessary for the
training of citizens capable of participating in society. Mill is
concerned with the freedom of individuals and the maintenance of a sphere of action secured against unwarranted
interference. The proponents of both these values, the liberty
of the individual and the social good, are not necessarily in
opposition to one another but can cooperate in the construction and maintenance of appropriate structures. But since
Vatican II's *Declaration on Religious Liberty*, the Catholic position
is no longer confined to its traditional reflection on law in

terms of the social good; it now also recognises the necessity of respect for the liberty of individuals as a ground for the limitation of the law's scope.[9]

CONCLUSION

In Chapter 4 I discussed the role of institutions in relation to the goods of practices and of public order. Part of the argument of subsequent chapters, including Chapter 5, is that the liberal, if she is to enjoy the freedoms associated with life in a liberal state, must foster both the institutions which sustain liberty and the personal values which support people's commitment to liberty. The minimalist, purely negative or reactive view of liberty is not sufficient if liberty is to be sustained. In this chapter I have argued for the need for a public space, at some distance from direct political controversy, in which it could be possible to conduct debate on those aspects of the common good relevant to politics. The need for this space in Irish political life has become evident from recent controversies. The space for debate about the law, that is, the space for considering what contributes to and what undermines public order, the stability of society, security and justice, is precarious. It is not to be taken for granted but needs to be sustained and protected. Perhaps the main threat to it is posed by those who collapse the distinction between morality and the civil law and attempt to derive proposals for the civil law from a substantive moral position. I have argued further that while some might be suspicious of the Catholic Church in Ireland as posing such a threat, they should seriously consider the developments which have taken place in the Catholic Church's understanding of politics and its recognition of the autonomy of a public space for debate.

CHAPTER 9

DISCOURSE AND THE PROCESS OF POLITICS

The need to secure a public space in which debate on issues of the good can take place was the concern of the previous chapter. I argued that there is a need for a forum which is insulated to some extent from the immediate issues and controversies of politics. Earlier chapters focused on the outline of the agenda for political debate in this broader sense, resisting tendencies to exclude questions of the good while recognising the limited perspective on the good appropriate to the public forum in a modern pluralist society. So the clarification of the meaning of public order can be seen as a setting of the agenda, and a securing of a space is partly achieved by the acceptance of that agenda. But what about the appropriate process for public debate: what is it and how might it be secured?

Traditionally, liberal thought has identified rational argument from agreed premises according to publicly acknowledged rules as the appropriate process. This process is relied upon to enable people who otherwise disagree fundamentally on the ultimate ends of action to agree to cooperate in political community. The liberal thinker's strategy is to seek reasons and criteria which can serve as common ground from which rational argument can proceed. Whether it be Hobbes on security, Locke on natural rights or Mill on liberty, each claims to be able to provide reasons acceptable to any challenger, why he might accept the authority of the state and cooperate

within it in handling conflict in a rational manner. This too is
the aim of contemporary liberal writers as for instance John
Rawls, whose work on justice and political liberalism is aimed
at finding a rational way to handle conflict. To be rational in
the handling of conflict is the dream of the Enlightenment
and the ideal appealed to by all advocates of liberal politics.

BARGAINING, NOT ARGUMENT

According to Alasdair MacIntyre, the typical procedure for
handling conflict in modern states is bargaining rather than
argument.[1] Bargaining, an exchange process in which there
is give and take, is the idiom appropriate to the marketplace.
It is ironic, on his view, that the form of state which explains
itself in terms of the rational handling of conflict exhibits
processes which are not linked in any way to argument.
Politicians who require the votes of constituents in order to
be elected offer deals in exchange for those votes, and parties
which require the support of other parties if they are to advance
their programmes engage in horse trading in order to generate
effective majorities. Governments are coalitions of interest
groups. Those who have nothing to bargain with are excluded
from the game of modern politics. Citizens who are deprived
of all other bargaining chips have at least their vote. The factor
of numbers becomes significant.[2] In liberal democratic politics,
it is not the strength of the better argument which counts, but
the ability to force those who control the levers of economic,
social and political power to negotiate. And to negotiate more
often than not means to bargain. That ability arises from the
control of some relevant source of power. Hence trades unions
created the countervailing power of an organised labour force,
obliging employers to enter procedures of collective bargaining. And minorities everywhere now know that if they are to
achieve a hearing for their concerns, they must organise.

THE IDIOM OF POLITICS

So central is the notion of interests and interest groups to the
idiom of contemporary politics that no constituency is now

without its single-issue candidate or party at election time. Local politics in particular is dominated by issues of local concern. The range of possible issues is enormous, from pot-holes to post offices. It is recognised that prisons are needed, but no one wants to live beside one. It is accepted that landfill dump sites are necessary, but that they should be located somewhere else. Clinics for drug addicts or for the treatment of sexually transmitted diseases are universally admitted to be appropriate to the state's response to relevant problems, but the public authorities encounter terrific local resistance whenever they propose to build or open one. Halting sites and houses among the settled community represent significant steps in addressing the issue of the travellers in Ireland, but there is almost universal objection to having them in one's own neighbourhood. The list of issues could be extended: incinerators, commercial ports, sewage treatment plants. The public campaigns associated with all of these issues reflect the same tension, namely, the tension between wanting something as good for our common life, and not being willing oneself to bear any of the personal costs of providing this good. The costs in question are usually identifiable and measurable. There is the drop in property values, the expense of installing security systems, the greater vigilance over children required when traffic increases or 'dangerous' characters frequent the area. Of course people do pay taxes and to this extent bear their share, equitable or otherwise, of the common burden. But the question of location means that the burden inevitably weighs more heavily on some than on others. And so we see all those campaigns which become vocal and influential in the planning process, in which local residents raise their objections to the public facility proposed for their area. The logic of the objections reveals that while the objectors are not willing themselves to accept the extra burden, they are willing that others should be asked to do so. Somebody has to pay, but let it be somebody else, not us.

How is such conflict to be regulated and how are solutions to be found? If planning laws and procedures effectively allow a veto to those who are organised and vocal enough to make their objections heard, then it seems that the groups in society who end up bearing the burden are those who are not organised and lack political clout. Where are the travellers' halting sites and the landfill dumps? They are seldom to be found in the areas in which local residents have organised and agitated. People are learning this lesson, of course, and all groups can now be expected to mobilise when their own interests are in jeopardy. If everybody can effectively say 'somebody must pay, but not us', then of course nobody will pay, and society will not get the facilities it needs to deal with its social problems. From the perspective of each individual or lobby group, their main concern is the securing of their own particular interest, and they can reassure themselves that the politicians and government officials will see to it that the problem is solved. After all, they may think, they are paying through their taxes for the services of the authorities. But what scope for action is left to government if it may not make demands on individuals and groups? If it does not have the possibility of requiring compliance by affected parties it can hardly act effectively in the public interest. Planning laws and procedures which are weighted in favour of objectors by allowing them effective vetoes do not well serve the wider political community. Procedures are required which enable solutions to common problems to be found, which do indeed allocate extra burdens to some.

I do not wish to imply that people ought not to be pursuing their interests in the political forum. The interests are real and are precisely the matters on which conflict arises and where decisions have considerable implications for people's lives. The point rather is that the processes of politics for handling the conflict are like forms of bargaining in which interest groups attempt to acquire positions of power from which they can exercise effective vetoes. The experience of this kind of political process confirms MacIntyre's juxtaposition of bargaining and argument. He sees them as being so different that the actual practice of liberal politics makes a mockery of the claims of the liberal theorist. While it is true that the processes of bargaining are a considerable advance on civil war, he maintains that they fall very short of the ideal of rational agreement which is claimed for them. And so in relation to fundamental conflicts in modern societies concerning the right to life, the distribution of property, and affirmative action to redress inequalities, MacIntyre maintains that it is not by argument from agreed principles that the disagreements are resolved. Rather, the democratic assemblies and the courts find some accommodation between the power blocks involved.[3]

In Chapter 2 I pointed out the difficulties which arise when attempts to explain and justify cooperation rely exclusively on models of rationality based on self-interest. Throughout the book I have been arguing for an alternative model of rationality and have been exploring the possibilities presented by a notion of the common good, and more specifically relative to state action, public order. But now the whole case for a politics of the common good seems jeopardised by the fact that the processes which operate in the politics of conflict are those appropriate to interests. So it is not sufficient to argue, as I did in the previous chapter, that there is need for a distinctive forum within which the concerns of the common good can be debated; it is also necessary to outline the appropriate processes for that debate and to show that it would be possible to sustain those processes in the face of the pressure towards bargaining.

The predominance of bargaining over rational argument in modern politics allowed MacIntyre to mock the claims of liberal thinkers in regard to the liberal state. While his use of the distinction between bargaining and argument seems valid, he is unfair in treating liberal thinkers in such a global manner. There is one contemporary thinker, very much in the liberal tradition, who is very conscious of the tension between bargaining and argument, and who addresses it in his writings. Jürgen Habermas, the German sociologist and philosopher, is associated with the notion of the communicative society, and with the idea of making social life more rational.[4] In this he is definitely within the tradition of the Enlightenment, but he is critical of the efforts of earlier thinkers to provide rational grounds for social order. The difficulty he sees with the projects of Hobbes or Locke, for instance, is that they identified what they considered to be the interests of any person, and proceeded to construct arguments which they judged would be acceptable to any rational person. There was no way of checking whether or not the identified interests were in fact common, and there was no procedure for getting the confirmation of rational approval from others. Habermas argues that there would have to be some such procedures if the promise of the Enlightenment thinkers were to be fulfilled. The main body of his own work has been to elaborate the conditions of an encounter between people who meet to deliberate on the issues which concern them, in such a way that they rely only on rational argument to achieve consensus.[5]

HABERMAS'S THEORY OF COMMUNICATIVE ACTION

Unlike those earlier writers in the liberal tradition who appealed to the content of particular interests in their search for common ground, Habermas explores what is presupposed in one activity exercised by all human beings, namely speech. We speak to one another, and our social interaction is made possible by speech. When we raise questions, make statements, query the assertions of others or commit ourselves to stated objectives, we appeal to criteria and standards which are normally taken for granted. These standards, which Habermas makes explicit in his theory, provide a common normative base for social existence.[6]

In debating about some matter which affects them, for instance the location of an incinerator for the disposal of waste in an urban area, participants express their own interests and concerns in public statements. The linguistic means which they use for the presentation of their interests oblige them to certain commitments, because of the validity claims implicit in the making of statements or raising of questions. For instance, assertions about the harmful effects of effluent carry the claim to truth. Someone making such assertions thereby also claims truth for his assertions, and undertakes to establish that truth if challenged. Similarly declarations of one's interest in the issue carry a claim to sincerity. Habermas also points to the way in which such statements or declarations are not isolated events, but are moves within recognisable patterns, such that they evoke typical responses from others. To make such a move is to enter into a process with others, and this involves its own commitment to respect the norms of the process. Argument therefore is a social interaction which relates people to one another in definite ways. In argument, various kinds of claims to validity are raised, and there is a mutual recognition of those claims. The obligation to provide justification for the different positions adopted is immanent in the speech-acts themselves.[7] In other words, it is not a matter of choosing to be rational, or choosing morality; one who engages in this kind of speech is already under obligation. A basic aspect of that obligation is reciprocity, akin to universalisability. This means that anyone who proposes a rule of action accepts to be bound by it himself, and undertakes to apply the rule equally to all others.[8] For instance, someone who insists that the problem of waste be avoided by recycling, but refuses to take the bother of recycling waste himself, cannot expect his proposal for others to be taken seriously.

We have been imagining a debate about waste disposal on which there is disagreement. The situation in which such debate could be handled rationally allows us to imagine an ideal situation and process. Habermas describes this ideal situation which he considers to be presupposed by all our attempts to enter into argument with one another. What is depicted in this idealised description is discourse. It makes explicit the implications of those claims which are implicit in our speech-acts. He formulates the rules for argument which make explicit our intuition of what it would mean to resolve conflict solely by the force of better argument. These rules do not directly indicate what is to be done so as to guarantee success, but they do provide criteria for identifying what might be wrong with the outcome of an already conducted debate. A first rule states that all those who are capable of speech and action are to be allowed to participate in discussions on practical matters which affect them. Just as the exclusion or suppression of some opinion might give us grounds for suspecting that the full truth has not been discovered because some lines of exploration have been blocked, so the exclusion of some people with their practical concerns might give us grounds for suspecting that the outcome of the deliberation cannot answer their possibly valid objections. So, for instance, if the local residents are not consulted in the decision to build an incinerator, we could suspect that their possibly valid concerns have not had an adequate airing, and the conclusion which ignored those concerns is unwarranted. And so there are further rules in order to ensure that none are excluded: each participant must be allowed, firstly, to call into question any proposal made by others, secondly, to introduce any proposal of his own into the discussion, and thirdly, to express his attitudes, wishes and needs. Corresponding therefore to these enabling rules which focus on allowing participation, there has to be a further general rule proscribing any measure of compulsion from whatever source which would prevent participation.[9] The exclusion of compulsion is essential for securing the required quality of discussion on practical matters, so that the absence of domination of whatever form ensures an atmosphere of freedom in the pursuit of a defensible solution. Of course, compulsion does not have to be a matter of physical force. It could also consist of a use of deception, power or ideology, whereby certain interests would be secured against demands for justification.

The ideal of discourse sets out what is entailed by the idea of being convinced by reason. The idealised participants in such discourse search for mutual understanding by offering arguments that could command assent. They attempt to convince each other by relying only on the force of the better argument. The conditions formulated by Habermas in his idealisation are such that only argumentative convincing is allowed to take place. The set of rules designed to guarantee equality, freedom and fair play in the discourse secures it against oppression and inequality. But oppression and inequality are always possibilities in real encounters between people. When questions are raised in the context of a conflict situation, either they are handled honestly, and a genuine search is conducted for an answer which satisfies and which can be defended against the objections of any affected person, or the process of questioning is blocked and some solution is imposed which requires the backing of force, since it cannot be defended against all criticism. This stark alternative, between solutions to problems which can be defended by argument and those solutions which require the defence of force, lays down the parameters of Habermas's analysis. In his terms they are contrasted as communicative action and strategic action.

Communicative Action versus Strategic Action

Communicative action, which is oriented to reaching a mutual understanding, is contrasted with strategic action, which is oriented to success. In strategic action people ask how they might succeed in furthering their own interests in situations in which the interests of others are also at stake. This is in contrast to the attitude of participants in discourse who ask how they might come to a understanding with those others in developing a position which all can accept as justified. The two types of activity reflect different models of rationality. Strategic action, oriented to success, applies the categories of means and goals to social affairs. From this perspective, other people and their interests appear either as obstacles to one's own goals, or as useful allies in the struggle. Intervention in social affairs is calculated to get others on one's side or to remove the obstacles they pose, so that one gets one's own way. Such intervention is guided by a technical calculation of the relation of means to goals which is different from the rationality reflected in a reasonable consensus. The rationality proper to the force of the better argument is thereby contrasted with the rationality of effectiveness and efficiency. And so the ideal of uncoerced agreement is contrasted with the possibility of manipulation whereby some succeed in advancing their own interests by using means other than the giving of reasons.

There is a tension in social and political life between these two ways of proceeding. The tendency to treat other people as either means or obstacles to one's own purposes encroaches more and more on social life the more society is subjected to bureaucratic regulation and control. Corresponding to the two kinds of rationality and the two kinds of action, Habermas draws a further distinction between these two dimensions of social life. In one dimension people encounter one another as partners in communication who can appeal to arguments in handling their difficulties. This dimension he refers to as the life-world. In another dimension, what Habermas calls social systems, social life is structured around routinised ways of coordinating behaviour. Social behaviour patterns exert pressure on individuals requiring them to conform but without any pretence of seeking the agreement of those affected. Habermas is thinking of the routines associated with various markets, with the organisation of work in the contemporary world, and with the operations of institutions. The logic of social systems is not that of the speech-act, but is a variation on the logic of strategic action. Habermas suggests that power and money are the basic terms in this way of thinking strategically.[10] In other words, someone wondering how to get other people to do what he wants will think of whether they can be paid to do it, or whether they can be made to do it. Threats, bribes and coercion are elements in the panoply of means, unrelated to the merits of an argument as such, which people rely on when acting strategically in order to bring about a desired result. Whenever the area governed by strategic action expands, the life-world contracts. The more the dynamics of the market intrude on human relations, the less possibility there is for deliberation about how those relations are to be structured. Hence Habermas's advocacy of discourse and communicative action in order to resist the powerful influences of social systems. The task he addresses is that of making social life more accessible to rational argument and critique; for this to succeed, the rationality of discourse must increasingly replace the rationality of means and goals.

A RATIONAL POLITICS?

The difficulties of relating Habermas's analysis of the ideal of discourse and the practice of politics in a modern state have been explored by Simone Chambers.[11] How can social and political life be made more rational in the sense of being imbued with the rationality of discourse? The task seems an impossible one, given the inherent tension between communicative and strategic action, and given the predominance of strategic action in the sphere of politics. Nonetheless the task is an important one, since the survival and stability of any political system depend not only on there being good reasons why citizens should cooperate in the system but also on those reasons being part of the normal self-understanding of citizens. In other words, it is not enough that some reasons exist to render legitimate the claims of a particular set of social and political structures: legitimacy by itself will not guarantee survival. It is also a necessary condition for the stability of a regime that those reasons which make it appear legitimate are known and recognised as such by a sufficient number of its participants. Political institutions cannot be maintained solely through force or strategic manipulation. That citizens have available to them reasons for cooperation is achieved through the communicative practice of people convincing one another that there really are good grounds to recognise as valid the demands made on them by the state. Without such a continuing process of providing and examining reasons, the shared background of acknowledgement and acceptance of the social and political world would disintegrate.[12]

It is this background function of discourse in a modern state which is important. It is clear that discourse is not very efficient as a way of making decisions, since the ideal of discourse is that it results in consensus grounded in the rational conviction of all participants. It would not be possible to achieve such consensus on most of the issues which divide people. There is an element of urgency in many problems such that one could not afford to wait for consensus to be achieved before doing something. How to dispose of waste is a typical example. But on the other hand, the various ways of terminating disputes, as for instance acceptance of a majority vote, or of judgments by courts or independent arbitrators, will not be acceptable to citizens unless they are situated within a broader context which is capable of commanding their assent. It is in the sustaining of this broader context that discourse has its place. It is a long-term consensus-building process which can contribute to making social life more rational. It is a process of education in which 'citizens build better foundations to their opinions through discursive interaction'.[13] Citizens become informed about the issues and about the positions taken up by others in relation to those issues. Argument and criticism can lead them to modify their own opinions, and so their conclusions become more reasoned. A sufficiently broad practice of discourse in a population ensures that public opinion is rooted in reasoned conviction, and this in turn ensures a certain quality in the exercise of democratic responsibility.

The practice of discourse contributes to making politics rational. How can it be sustained? Institutional supports can be created and maintained in order to facilitate this practice. For instance, the guarantees of freedom of speech and freedom of the press are intended to exclude those obstacles which would prevent open debate. But such institutional supports cannot ensure that open debate in fact takes place. Nor can they ensure that the agenda of debate includes the questions of legitimacy or the grounds for compliance and obedience. As Chambers points out, there can be no legal requirement that participants in debate listen to what others have to say, that they attempt to understand the other's point of view, that they refrain from manipulating or deceiving, and that they allow themselves to be swayed only by the force of the better argument.[14] Discourse will always be under pressure from a strategic way of thinking. To the extent that it exists at all, it will always coexist with reliance on negotiation, instrumental trade-offs, and strategic bargaining in handling disputes. Habits of debate which are developed within the contexts of the marketplace and institutions of conflict resolution such as the law courts will be the greatest obstacle to the practice of discourse. Such conversational habits will prove

to be the source of resistance to a more rational social interaction.[15]

Chambers applies Habermas's ideas to contemporary
politics by discussing four questions. Her questions and answers
provide me with a useful structure for my purposes. First of all
she asks what the practice of discourse is supposed to accomplish. She suggests that it should contribute to making public
opinion and decision making more rational. To a second
question why it is important that we engage in such a practice,
she answers that the dual values of justice and stability in
political institutions can be realised only if people in fact have
good reasons for believing that those institutions are legitimate. The third question asks what would be required of
people if they do engage in such a practice. To this she answers
that they would have to strive to be discursive rather than
strategic actors. That is to say, they would have to exhibit the
qualities of listening and speaking appropriate to finding and
being bound by the better argument. The final question asks
about the link between the practice of discourse and
democratic politics. The answer given is that discourse has a
limited but essential role in democratic decision making. This
is because discourse has no mechanism for ending a debate
and identifying a conclusion as final; there is always the
possibility of new experience and a further question. It is the
third question which is relevant to my concerns. It points to
the qualities which participants would have to exhibit if their
interaction were to approximate to discourse rather than
strategic manipulation. Participants would have to adopt
attitudes of equal respect and impartiality. They would have
to be prepared to treat one another as equal partners, giving
each other the opportunity to speak. But they would also have
to listen and respond to one another, and be prepared to justify
their positions. These attitudes express the kind of respect for
one another which would be a precondition of discourse.
Chambers emphasises the internal nature of these conditions.
They cannot be legislated for or commanded.[16]

THE PROCESS AS A COMMON GOOD

It is now possible to relate this discussion to the earlier presentation of MacIntyre and to the topic of this book. It is noticeable that Chambers uses the notion of practice when presenting and elaborating Habermas's understanding of discourse. She does not explain what she means by practice, but it is clear from her usage that her meaning for the term is consistent with that presented by MacIntyre. Recall that for him a practice is any complex and coherent form of socially established activity in which people cooperate in the pursuit of internal goods.[17] The kind of discourse which Chambers discusses is a practice in this sense. The internal goods which are pursued cooperatively in the practice of discourse are truth and validity, as well as the excellent performance achieved by contributors to the discussion. The coincidence in the use of the same term by both MacIntyre and Chambers is not purely linguistic: there is a concurrence in their meanings as well. Another point at which the thought of these two authors converges is in relation to virtues. Where MacIntyre understands virtues as acquired qualities which enable people to achieve the internal goods which they pursue in practices, Chambers underlines the internal preconditions of discourse. Her listing of the internal attitudes which participants would have to have if their interaction with one another in debate were to approximate to discourse is in fact a listing of virtues in MacIntyre's sense. The readiness to relinquish manipulative interventions, the willingness to allow others their opportunity to speak and to grant them a respectful hearing, and the submission to the discipline of accepting the better argument are acquired qualities which would tend to enable people to achieve the truth and validity which they pursue in the practice of debate.

These connections in terms of practices and virtues are interesting. But more important perhaps is the way in which Chambers manages to suggest how the practice of discourse could be related to the processes of politics in a modern state. Where MacIntyre sees practices and politics as polar opposites, Chambers recognises the necessary contribution of the practice of discourse to the survival of politics. MacIntyre considers that practices and the virtues could only be at home in local, small-scale community, and that the modern state with its typical concern for the public interest is inhospitable to practices. Argument and bargaining are incompatible opposites. Chambers also recognises that the decision-making processes in a modern state would be unlikely to exhibit the qualities of discourse. However, she argues that those decision-making processes will not command widespread acceptance unless they are rooted in a background context which is sustained by the practice of discourse, in the demanding and giving of reasons for compliance. For her, argument and bargaining are indeed different, but not incompatible; there must be a practice of argument in the background if bargaining is to be stable and just as a way of handling disputes in the forefront of politics. Her claims for the contribution of the practice of discourse to politics are modest therefore. They are not the overly optimistic claims of the Enlightenment, which invite the criticisms of MacIntyre.

Finally, in relation to the topic of this book, this discussion allows us to specify one more element of the common good of liberal politics. Citizens may well pursue different ends and may disagree on what constitutes a good life; but they can have a common interest in there being a state which respects their liberties, which does not favour the interests of some over others, and which guarantees some measure of security and protection. This will be part of their common good. Also they can have a common interest in there being a forum in which they can meet to debate their differences, at some remove from the day-to-day controversies of politics. But now it is also clear that the availability of the forum is not sufficient to ensure that the desired debate will be conducted along the lines of discourse. There is the additional requirement that participants bring to the encounter the willingness and internal attitudes without which discourse will not take place. Accordingly, it will be part of the common good of concerned citizens in a liberal state that the practice of discourse be fostered, and that participants acquire the necessary willingness and attitudes for conducting argument. Concretely this will mean not only a concern about the institutional means of excluding threats to open discussion, such as the protection of the freedom of speech, but more positively a concern for the quality of education of citizens in the practice of argument. What examples are available to people on which they can model their own performance of argument, how they are facilitated at every level in entering into discourse, and how communicative action might be reinforced in preference to strategic action in the education of children would all be appropriate and likely issues of concern.

CONCLUSION

Habermas provides a double service. On the one hand, he formulates the elements involved in a rational handling of disputes. He provides criteria for validating achieved consensus as defensible. These provide us with a depiction of the process appropriate to the conducting of rational discourse. But on the other hand, Habermas also provides a critique of the actual processes which operate in our economic and political systems. Those processes are dominated by manipulative relationships in which money and power are the typical factors at play in the technical domain of means. On the one hand, he is an Enlightenment philosopher, committed to achieving emancipation by reliance on rational means. On the other hand, he is the incisive critic, exposing the deceits of contemporary liberal economic and political systems.

Simone Chambers's development of his thought shows the relevance of the practice of discourse to the stability of a political system. Discourse could not replace the bargaining and other procedures appropriate to decision making in politics, but on the other hand, these would become unstable if they lacked the background support of legitimacy as sustained by discourse. Her discussion also emphasises that discourse is a precarious process, which is always in jeopardy and likely to deteriorate into strategic action. Advocacy of the process for the sake of making social life more rational requires commitment to creating those conditions which are necessary if communicative action is to be realised in political life.

MacIntyre's juxtaposition of argument and bargaining parallels Habermas's distinction of communicative and strategic action. Even if they differ in their attitudes to the Enlightenment agenda, MacIntyre being sceptical of it while Habermas continues to represent it, they both point to the precarious nature of the processes for a rational handling of conflict. These are always in danger of being corrupted into manipulation while wearing the aura and claiming the justification of rationality. To secure those processes requires that attention be focused, not merely on the elements of talking which is to qualify as rational, but also on the characters of speakers who are to be capable of rational debate. And so it must be an element of the common good for any political culture which aims at handling its conflict by talking, to find and foster the people capable of such talking. Where do they come from, how are they to be trained, what will be their motivation, what will be their values and how might those values be sustained, especially where there is the danger of seduction by external goods or by the currency of social systems? The securing of the process by measures oriented to answering these questions concretely is part of the common good of citizens who cooperate in maintaining a political culture based on communicative action.

In Chapter 7 I discussed the role which an understanding of the human good could play in the common good of citizens in a liberal state. There I emphasised the notion of human flourishing in the exercise of certain functions and that the recognition of those functions as central to being able to live well could allow a role for the liberal state in relation to the human good. It would have an interest in providing the material and institutional conditions which would allow people to develop and exercise their capacities for participation in social and political life. The discussion in this chapter of the importance of discourse and of the internal conditions for discourse reinforces that earlier conclusion about the human good. It can and to some extent must be part of the common good of a liberal political system that its citizens exercise their autonomy as participants in the practice of discourse.

CHAPTER 10

THE LANGUAGE OF THE COMMON GOOD

T he discussion of the idea of public order in the preceding chapters can be seen as an attempt to break out of the restrictions of the polarisation between self-interest and a broader conception of the human good. There is a way of thinking associated with each of these poles. Those ways of thinking can be presented in theoretical models of practical rationality. Such models are available, but my argument has been that to adopt a model based exclusively on self-interest is to limit considerably what can be explained, and a model based on a view of the unrestricted human good is not practicable for explanation because of the lack of consensus on this good. What is needed, I have suggested, is a model of practical rationality which will allow us to encompass the full spectrum of human interaction which ranges from cases of conflict, in which common ground has to be established, to cases of cooperation, in which there is already some consensus. The question I have posed is whether we can express a rationality for this whole spectrum without subscribing to the minimum interest assumptions of the conflict cases, and without postulating some special type of interest like altruism. The task is not simply theoretical. If we have experience of social cooperation across this broad spectrum from conflict to consensus, then it must be the case that people can cooperate, and so the task is to articulate the practical rationality which is implicit in their activity.

My proposal is that the notion of the common good can

serve this purpose. Earlier chapters discussed the content of this notion in considering practices and institutions (Chapter 4), public order (Chapters 5 and 6), the dimensions of the human good of concern to all citizens of a liberal state (Chapter7), and the appropriate forum and procedure for the encounter of citizens in debate with one another (Chapters 8 and 9). In this chapter it remains to spell out the language of the common good in order to see its strengths and weaknesses as an element of the overlapping consensus. My claims for the language of the common good must now be elaborated and tested, at least to the very limited extent of seeing if this is a fruitful direction for further investigation.

On first sight it seems an implausible claim, because of the range of meanings given to the term common good in various theoretical models. There can be the virtual denial of the reality of any distinct common good along with the assertion that the public interest is identical with the facilitation of private interests; there can be the assertion of some restricted purpose as the common good of political community, as for instance internal and external security, or the protection of property, or the enforcement of contracts; there can be the utilitarian summation of private interests under the heading of general welfare, viewed as a counterpole to the claims of individuals; there can be the comprehensive vision of human fulfilment articulated as a good for any human person, and therefore a good common to all. Are these different meanings inevitably contradictory, or is there a possibility of integrating them in a unified understanding which allows the distinctiveness of each conception to be retained?

The phrase common good can be used to refer to the comprehensive and unrestricted good, whether understood in a philosophical or a theological context. Or it can be used to refer to a minimal condition for the existence of public order and society and political authority. Which is the appropriate meaning for the term when applied to the operations of the modern democratic state? And when politicians or political parties or public servants are accused of neglecting the common good, in which sense of the term ought the accusation be considered? When it is asserted that there is a lack of commitment to the common good in Irish politics today, which sense is meant?

There is another problem with the meaning of the concept. How can people be sure that the rhetoric appealing to the interests of all is not a cloak for the interests of some? It may be the case that people have good reasons for ignoring the claims of the common good, in whichever sense, and for concentrating on their private interests. Many people may find themselves asked to carry a disproportionate burden in the name of the general welfare, or the common good. I suspect there has been repeated experience over time to confirm some people in the view that the common good usually refers to somebody else's good, because they have so rarely seen the sacrifices they have made in its name as in any way benefiting them. One would not be surprised therefore to find that people on the margins of the economy and society such as the unemployed and the low paid are reluctant to set aside the pursuit of their immediate interests for the sake of the common good.

How is the common good to be understood, so that it genuinely is a *common* good, and not the sectional good of political parties or social elites or administrators or beneficiaries? How can there be a genuine *common* good, when there are not only diverse interests in society, but interests which are opposed to one another? What has to happen in order that such a properly understood common good can become the basis for new forms of cooperation in politics?

The Return to Aristotle

In the range of possible meanings for the common good listed above, Aristotle's is included at one end of the spectrum. But in fact Aristotle would have understood his discussion not simply as one position among others, but as providing the necessary distinctions and categories for a consideration of a range of views. In other words, Aristotle would claim to have provided a scheme with which it is possible to compare political constitutions with one another in terms of their views of the human good and their conceptions of justice. This aspect of his thought gives it a perennial relevance, and it is not surprising to find that several authors today draw on Aristotle in the context of the discussion of the advantages and limitations of liberal political constitutions.[1] One of the key concepts which Aristotle uses for his analysis is that of friendship, and this too is enjoying renewed interest on the part of political philosophers.[2]

John Finnis offers an updated version of Aristotle on the common good.[3] His approach to this topic is via Aristotle's distinctions between the different types of friendship. These types of friendship exhibit different kinds of goods to be achieved through cooperation, and the distinction between types of goods reflects distinctions between reasons which people can have for cooperating. Finnis presents a theoretical analysis of cooperation in terms of reasons, but at the same time he intends it to be an articulation of the kinds of reasons which are in fact operative in people's interaction. He takes the orientations of practically engaged and committed people as primary and attempts to reflect them in his theory.

Why people in fact cooperate, and why they ought to cooperate with one another, cannot be explained without reference to the reasons which they themselves can give to explain and justify their action. The expression 'common good' is a useful tag for referring to those reasons which people have for cooperating with one another. The common good is not some identifiable or measurable content, as might be implied by a utilitarian emphasis on the 'greatest good of the greatest number'. Rather, its reality is the actual sharing of purposes and concerns by people who are involved in joint action. Appeal to the common good is therefore contingent. The effectiveness of the appeal depends on there being reasons which do in fact give those addressed grounds for cooperating with others. Obviously, there are also psychological and sociological conditions which contribute to this contingency: for instance, the people addressed must be capable of recognising their own interests, and the social means of communication must be effective in allowing the message to be heard. However, the contingency I wish to point to here is that the reasons adverted to in the appeal to the common good may not in fact be held by those addressed. If they do not have the opportunity to declare what their own interests are, and accordingly to specify which of their interests are shared with others and are therefore a common good, then any appeal for their cooperation in the name of the common good is likely to be manipulative.

The common good identifies the point of continuing cooperation. It refers to the answers which people might give to questions like: 'why do you go along with that crowd, why do you continue to go to those meetings, why do you continue to work with them, why do you let them do that, why do you not stop them, why do you pay your contribution to that organisation?' The people involved must themselves be able to say what the point of their common activity is; their common good is something which, ideally, they themselves could identify, rather than something proposed to them from outside.

What kinds of reasons do people typically have for co-operating with one another? Finnis answers this question by distinguishing various forms of cooperation. Corresponding to each of these forms is a distinctive set of reasons, a particular kind of answer to the question why. Aristotle's distinction of the different types of friendship – of utility, of pleasure and of pure friendship – is reformulated in a distinction of business relations, play relations and friendship. Finnis adds a fourth, which he calls complete community. These forms of cooper-ation are distinguished according to the various attitudes people may have towards the goals of others with whom they are involved. There can be cooperation where there is either no interest in or even opposition to the goals of partners (busi-ness relations); there can be partial interest in the other's goals as in the form of cooperation where the partner's successful performance is valued as a condition for one's own success (play relations); and there can be commitment to the goals of the other on a par with one's own ambitions (friendship).

Business Relations

It is a familiar element in our experience that we cooperate with people we do not know, that we cooperate with people about whose goals we know nothing and in fact care less, and surprisingly, that we cooperate with people with whom we are in competition, that is, whose goals are at variance with our own. We cooperate in such instances, because there is some good valued by all the people involved, no matter how much they may differ otherwise. Those who come to a market to buy and sell have opposed interests: if the sellers do well, then it is at the expense of the buyers, and vice versa. But even though they have opposed interests, buyers and sellers cooperate in maintaining the market and its arrangements: place, time, auctioneering facilities. Here they have a common good, although their other goals are not shared. Many other forms of joint action reflect a willingness to similar cooperation in the presence of ultimate disinterest in the goals of others. In a well-coordinated traffic system, for instance, it is in the interests of each to comply with the regulations for the sake of efficiency in achieving her own goals; each would have an interest in the cooperation of all, without being concerned in the least with the goals pursued by others. Whether they are driving to work, to school, to shop, or to rendezvous with their lovers is of no concern to the other participants in the traffic, only that they comply with the rules of the road. These instances of cooperation involve some measure of common interest, but all in the service of each participant attaining her own objective.[4] The objective of each remains individual and private; the success of any one is a matter of indifference to others, and the coordination of action is not valued by anyone as a component of her own objective.[5]

Finnis's discussion can be illustrated in terms of the example, discussed in Chapter 4, of the college chess club, the finance committee, and the institutions which sustain these. Those who participate in the deliberations of the college finance committee perhaps represent different concerns, whether those of the college administration, or of the various student organisations with their distinctive activities. More money for the chess club means less for the drama society, or some other body. There is competition, but still there is cooperation in operating the structures of the finance committee. Valued as an arrangement which allows various groups to pursue their different goods, it is sustained and operated because those participating do in fact share this common good.

PLAY RELATIONS

In other forms of cooperation the people involved share some goals and the answers they would give to a question about their willingness to continue to participate would point to those goals. In play relations, Aristotle's friendship of pleasure, people engage in joint activity for the sake of the enjoyment to be derived from that activity. Sport provides the clearest example. If I play well, I can enjoy a game of tennis, but I can only play well if my opponent also plays well and gives me a good game. Even though we are competing to win the tennis match, we play tennis for the enjoyment this form of sport provides, and so the interest in playing well and having a good game is more basic than the interest in winning. The love of the game is hardly realised by too-easy wins or no-contest matches. In such forms of cooperation, the success of the other in achieving her goal is a condition for me achieving mine. The coordination of activity, the performance itself, is valued by the participants for its own sake, and is a significant part of their common good.[6] MacIntyre's example of the pursuit of the internal goods of chess can also serve to illustrate this form of friendship and cooperation. Members of the chess club may not have any dealings with one another beyond their common interest in chess, but in this area they will be concerned for the quality of one another's performance.

FRIENDSHIP

When one or other of us has improved at the game and we no longer give one another a satisfactory match, it is not at all unusual that we could look around for more suitable partners. In play relations the partner is of interest only to the limited extent of our joint action. But in more extensive relationships like friendship, my willingness to cooperate with the other is not made to depend on performance or other conditions. Where there is friendship in this fuller sense, I am interested in my friend's well-being for her own sake; my friend's realisation of the chosen set of goals that makes up her plan of life becomes a constitutive part of my own well-being. Familial relationships can fit into this category as well as the more formal friendships. The concern of parents for the well-being of their children is such that the flourishing of the children is a constitutive part of the parents' well-being. Husbands and wives engage in joint activity which has as its common good their mutual fulfilment and the realisation of their life's projects. The interest in the other's goals is not confined to only one aspect of cooperation, but extends to the whole range of the partner's good. Friends are interested not just in their own success, in the maintenance of conditions of cooperation, or in successful coordination. They are interested in the other's success as a constitutive part of their own well-being, and so the common good of friends in their shared activity is their mutual fulfilment.

MacIntyre's example of the chess club cannot provide an illustration of friendship in the complete sense, because of the limited focus of the goods involved. But MacIntyre also suggested the example of a fishing community in which people pursued the common good of a life of excellence as crew member and exponent of the craft of fishing. As noted above in Chapter 4, the bond of unity in such communities is a shared vision and understanding of some good.[7] Their good, in this sense the common good, includes all the goods internal to the relevant practices, the goods of lives of a certain kind, and the goods of communities in which the practices are fostered. He speaks of 'the shared making and sustaining of the types of community within which the common good can be achieved – families, farming households, fishing crews, local forms of political community'.[8] These examples can be taken to illustrate Finnis's presentation on friendship as rooted in a care for the well-being of others as an integral part of one's own well-being.

COMPLETE COMMUNITY

The question of the common good does not arise primarily in terms of economic or sporting or intimate relationships, but in relation to political community. What is to be understood by the common good of political community? Finnis follows Aristotle again here. Aristotle explains the emergence of the *polis* in the evolution of community in terms of the insufficiency of the lesser forms for achieving the human good; the *polis* is that level of social organisation at which a community can be said to be self-sufficient in providing the good life for itself.[9] Households and villages cannot provide all that is needed for the maintenance of the good life in all its aspects. Similarly, isolated instances of cooperation on the model of business relations, play relations or friendship cannot exhaust all the potential for the realisation of the goods for the sake of which people would have reason to cooperate. And so Finnis introduces the notion of complete community to characterise that level of social organisation which is oriented to the unrestricted range of the good. He challenges the prevalent assumption that the sovereign nation state is such complete community. This assumption is based on a transference of the attributes of Aristotle's *polis* to the nation state. In fact, international cooperation is required to deal with problems of an environmental, economic, cultural and ideological as well as technological nature. Complete community, like friendship, is never an achieved state of affairs, but something to be striven for. It involves patterns of cooperation which transcend the divisions of states, but which include sovereign states as actors in the cooperation.

The analysis of this form of cooperation does not require an extra model however, as complete community can be explained as a complex amalgam of forms of cooperation which are instances of business relations, play relations and friendship. Anyone's activity as a citizen or politician can be understood in one or more of these ways. The citizen who cooperates in abiding by the traffic laws or tax laws may see this as part of a deal made with other citizens, whereby each stands to gain from the established order. The reasoning

behind their cooperation would then conform to the model
of business relations. Traditional social contract philosophies
of the state have used this model to clarify the rationality of
political community. Each citizen is willing to forgo some
liberties on condition that all other citizens do so too, for the
sake of the security and stability which such an arrangement
would bring about.[10]

The model of play relations can also explain political activity.
Those who take part in political life can be motivated partly
by the enjoyment they derive from the power play. There is a
'pay-off' which those of a political inclination enjoy: popularity,
success in swaying meetings, skill in negotiating and forming
alliances. The enjoyment of the give and take of political
debate, of the access to the levers of power which political
office allows, of the influence over events which politicians
invariably enjoy, reflects the possibility of understanding
some dimensions of political activity on the model of play
relations.

Thirdly, the model of friendship can be a significant element
in explaining human cooperation in political affairs. By this is
meant not the friendships which statesmen and politicians may
form with one another, but the genuine concern for the well-
being of others for their own sake which motivates some people
to struggle for the creation and maintenance of democratic
systems, of rule according to law, of adequate health care and
social welfare and education systems. If there were not this
form of motivation for participation in political activity, then
our political societies would truly conform to the image of
shepherd and sheep, whereby the shepherds take care of the
sheep, but only for the purpose of fattening them for
slaughter.[11] The ingenuity and competence which have gone
into the organisation of the various elements of government
and the social services could not have been motivated alone
by desire for the kind of goods achievable in business and
play relations. And indeed societies traditionally recognise
their duty to say thank you to those who have contributed to
the public welfare, recognising that the salaries paid to officials
and the gratification to be had from participation are hardly

sufficient to acknowledge the struggles and the commitment which public service has involved. The relationships which exist in political community are not only characterised by private interest which would motivate relations of a business nature; they are not only characterised by the enjoyment of participation which would motivate relations of play; they also include relations of friendship, where the motivation is the well-being of others who stand to benefit from the institutions and operations of politics.[12]

The common good of complete community is a complex amalgam of the three types of common good appropriate to the more specialised forms of cooperation. The reasons which anyone might give for participating in and contributing to political activity can range across these three basic models. Accordingly, the common good of complete community would identify a complex set of conditions allowing each, by her cooperation, to realise her own good; further it would include a set of typical operations by participation in which each would enhance her own well-being; but finally it would include a vision of the well-being of all the members of the community, achieved by their own intelligent and responsible pursuit of their own life-plans, facilitated by the structures and institutions of the community.

APPLICATION OF FINNIS'S ANALYSIS

The advantage of John Finnis's analysis is that it permits us to see the point of the other approaches to the common good without being trapped in the restrictions of any particular understanding. Understandings can be located along a spectrum. Those who view the common good of political community in a minimalist sense or even deny any distinctive common good as such can be seen as interpreting society exclusively on the model of business relations. Those who advocate a comprehensive common good incorporating a moral vision can be seen as interpreting society exclusively on the model of friendship. Each approach has its validity, as is clear from our experience. But if either is elevated to the central role in explaining social relations, the relevance of the other dimensions of human cooperation is overlooked.

THE ANALOGICAL CONCEPTION OF THE COMMON GOOD

Finnis's analysis of complete community as an amalgam of forms of cooperation, including instances of business relations, play relations and friendship in its various degrees, makes it possible to acknowledge the validity of specialised views. With this approach, firstly, the appropriateness of the minimal social contract to guarantee security, protection of basic rights, and liberties for individual actors can be acknowledged. At the same time, secondly, the importance of participation in political community as constitutive of human flourishing is given its due place. And thirdly, it is recognised that without the friendship which makes sense of a commitment to the well-being of others, political community as such would hardly survive.

THE MINIMUM IS NOT ENOUGH

If self-interest is to provide the only motivation for socially significant activity, and the market is to be the only nexus of social interaction, then it is clear that political community will function to ensure that the wealthy and the strong survive. Adequate health care, legal protection, education, the necessities of life would not be provided for all, since there are many who have nothing to trade and so have nothing to offer those who might be able to help them.

WHO PREFERS THE MINIMALIST VIEW?

Usually those who are benefiting from the system of cooperation in the body politic and the economy give special place to the business relations aspect of social cooperation. The rights to property, civil liberties, the legal enforcement of contract, along with the maintenance of a certain type of law and order are part of the structure which allows them to achieve their own private goals. Is it mistaken to suggest that this group will usually include the wealthy and powerful? When such people rely on the rhetoric of the common good, they draw on the vocabulary of affection and friendship, of loyalty and gratitude, which properly belongs to political community in the full sense. But though they draw on this rhetoric, they exploit it to evoke commitment to a restricted view of political association, namely, one based on business relations.

'What's In It For Us?'

Minority groups, the poor and the less well off who are frequently asked to accept sacrifices in the name of the common good, though they are addressed in the expansive language of friendship, are quite entitled to ask the question, rooted in the restricted model of business relations, 'what's in it for us?' Jean Jacques Rousseau has commented that a political community begins to disintegrate as soon as the citizens begin to ask 'What's in it for us?'[13] Service of the community rather than exploitation of the common wealth is the life blood of political community in his view. But although his argument is persuasive, it depends on the presupposition that there exists a basic equality among the citizens. Where this equality does not exist, and furthermore, where those in a vulnerable minority position or in the socially worse-off position have good reasons to suspect they may lose out in the future as they have lost in the past, then they are well justified in asking what's in it for them. This question pushes in the direction of a more comprehensive vision of the common good, in which the well-being of each member and each section of the community is taken seriously. The distribution of housing, jobs, schooling, health care, even food, can effectively map out the reality of the common good. Those who are faring badly in these terms can very reasonably challenge others in the community, and especially those with control over resources and therefore with responsibility, to show evidence of their commitment to the common good.

Suppose people are being invited to act for the well-being of others out of a spirit of friendship towards them; they would be foolish to respond unless the first level of cooperation is realised, that is, the form of political community which guarantees them security, a living, the protection of their rights. Those who wish to advocate a culture of the common good must work so as to persuade people, through the concreteness of their own experience, that they are not like the sheep who are being looked after for the sake of the profit to be made from them. Commitment to the common good can only be expected from people who have had the experience that their own good is seriously taken into consideration by others, but especially by those explicitly charged with responsibility for the common good.

THE MAXIMUM IS NOT POSSIBLE

Just as at one extreme in a spectrum of meanings of the common good, the minimum is not enough, so at the other extreme, the maximum is not possible. The realisation of the comprehensive common good would be heaven, and this is not within the gift of any human society or any state. The genuine alternative to the minimalist conception of the common good, modelled on business relations, is therefore a more comprehensive view which includes elements of friendship, while stopping short of the paternalism which would take complete responsibility for the destinies of people. It is a matter of providing the conditions which make it possible for people, by their own initiative and activity, to achieve their own fulfilment. Or in the words of *Gaudium et Spes*, 'the common good embraces the sum total of all those conditions of social life which enable individuals, families and organisations to achieve complete and efficacious fulfilment'.[14] The common good of political community as envisaged in this definition is less than the complete fulfilment of its members: rather it is the set of conditions which allows those members to identify and pursue their own fulfilment.

It is to be hoped that the wide-ranging discussion of this chapter helps to clarify the meaning and usefulness of a language of the common good. The reasons which people can have for cooperating will be complex, just as the forms of human associating are varied, and the range of goals and values to be realised in coordinated activity is extensive. The concept of the common good is not simply empirical, reporting what happen to be the reasons operative in actual instances of social cooperation, but it is also a normative concept, since those who use it are also faced with the practical question about the forms of political community which they would wish to construct and operate. Those who react sceptically to appeals to the common good may be quite justified in their scepticism, because of previous experience of being asked to make sacrifices in relation to their own interests, without compensatory benefits. On the other hand, those who rely on an expansive rhetoric of the common good in order to motivate the cooperation of others, without at the same time moving in practice beyond a self-interested involvement rooted in the business relations models, are to be challenged for the deceitfulness of their position. The rhetoric of the common good can be manipulative unless it is substantiated by activity rooted in the friendship model of cooperation and political community. While the minimalist view of the common good is not sufficient for the maintenance and survival of political community, the maximalist view is not a practicable option. Some intermediate model is more appropriate, which combines elements of business relations, focusing on security and self-interest, with elements of play relations (participation as a value) and especially friendship, whereby the commitment to the well-being of others is a significant aspect of the practical rationality of citizens and politicians. The understanding of conflict as an unavoidable aspect of political community is compatible with this model of the common good, and so politics is freed from the demand for consensus and harmony.

CONCLUSION

The opening chapter discussed punishment as an illustration of the impact different models could have on the way in which this social phenomenon is perceived and understood. The contrast was drawn between models which assumed conflict between individuals whose interests were incompatible with one another, and models which assumed a certain communality of interest and activity. Also a question about the working credos actually operative in the activities of professionals in the penal system pointed to the need for explicit reflection on the models we rely upon for thinking about our experience. I argued that the reliance on models assuming conflict between isolated individuals would in fact contribute to us both interpreting and constructing social interaction in those terms. This would be a self-fulfilling prophecy, leading to a diminishment in social cohesion. While noting the importance of distinguishing between articulated models used in theory, and the models operative in our everyday activity, I argued that it would be foolish to continue to pretend that the articulated models are merely descriptive, or merely tools of analysis. They do in fact feed in to how we make sense of our world, and how we go about shaping it.

The questions I raised in relation to the relatively confined domain of punishment serve as examples for questions which are relevant to us as citizens in relation to the much broader domain of political culture and debate. Examination of the model of rationality based on the assumption of self-interest revealed how this model subtly determines what is to qualify as a reason in public debate. Identification of the limitations of self-interest pointed in the direction of the need for analyses which allow for communality, or shared or common interests. In the course of my discussion of those limitations, I elaborated the notion of public order which would be the common good of politics. While I argued that public order would have to include more than the minimal shared interests presupposed by traditionally liberal analyses, it would not include a comprehensive treatment of the human good.

Other discussions led me to conclude that social institutions can be valued as common goods, because of the way in which they enable people and groups to achieve the internal goods which they seek in practices. But furthermore I argued that these institutions could not be relegated simply to the realm of means, since some at least of the institutions essential to aspects of public order are elements of the ends which people pursue in cooperation with one another. And so the common good of political community would include the maintenance of a space for debate on aspects of the human good, and it would include the maintenance of conditions to ensure a certain quality of participation in that debate, so that it would not deteriorate finally into mere bargaining. The conditions to be maintained would have to include the capacities of citizens for participation in discourse free from domination, and the forms of education and training to develop those capacities. Again this consideration brought the line of thought back to the issue of the human good, and the possibility of elaborating thick, vague descriptions of human goods, even in the context of disagreement on fundamental religious, moral and philosophical convictions. Many of the pointers offered in support of the argument that we require a model which presupposes a common good are inconclusive and require further development. However, I hope they are sufficiently cogent to support my optimism that we can generate meaningful models with more than minimalist presuppositions about our acting in cooperation with one another.

My argument can be summarised in the following few sentences: we have to think about how we think about our social interaction. How we have been taught to think about it (by the economic and social sciences for instance) leads us to act in ways which undermine social cohesion. But our social experience reveals possibilities of achievement of goods which we value, and of forms of activity which enrich us all. If we want these goods and these opportunities of participation, should we continue to think and speak and therefore also act in ways which jeopardise those goods? And it seems there might be alternative ways of thinking about human cooperation which are more true to all aspects of our experience. We do have common goods, even where we disagree on fundamental matters. Having a language which makes it possible for us to talk about the goods we have in common would make it more likely that we could build forms of cooperation with one another. And this is something which is central to the liberal and Enlightenment concern, that we would handle our conflict by rational means. So I hope to have shown that a language of the common good need not be sectarian in the sense mentioned in the Introduction, but that it can be central to a constructive liberal approach to contemporary politics.

NOTES TO CHAPTERS

INTRODUCTION

1. John Rawls, *Political Liberalism* (New York: Columbia University Press, 1993).
2. Pope John Paul II, *Evangelium Vitae* (Dublin: Veritas, 1995), especially paras. 70–72.
3. See. 'Sect', *Dictionary of Theology* (New York: Crossroad, new revised edition, 1981), edited by K. Rahner and H. Vorgrimler, p. 469.
4. Attracta Ingram, *A Political Theory of Rights* (Oxford: Oxford University Press, 1994), p. 118.
5. Ibid., p. 150.
6. Ibid., p. 4.

CHAPTER 1: THE COMMON GOOD: LOCATING THE PROBLEM

1. I am using the edition of the *Discourse on the Origins of Inequality* reproduced in *Classics of Moral and Political Theory,* edited by Michael L. Morgan (Indianapolis, Indiana: Hackett, 1992). The quotation is from Part I of the *Discourse,* p. 873.
2. Bill Jordan, *The Common Good* (Oxford: Blackwell, 1989).
3. Andrew Rutherford, *Criminal Justice and the Pursuit of Decency* (Oxford: Oxford University Press, 1993).
4. Ibid., p. 11.
5. Ibid.
6. Ibid., p. 13.
7. Rutherford quotes Tony Bottoms, 'An Introduction to "The Coming Penal Crisis"', in A. E. Bottoms and R. H. Preston (eds.), *The Coming Penal Crisis* (Edinburgh: Scottish Academic Press, 1980), p. 2.

8. Rutherford, *Criminal Justice*, p. 29.
9. By humane values he means the 'cluster of values that manifest themselves in empathy and respect for the offender, an optimism that people can make progress with their lives, and an insistence upon justice and on clear lines of accountability to democratic institutions'. Ibid., p. xi.
10. See for example R. J. Gerber and P. D. McAnany (eds.), *Contemporary Punishment: Views, Explanations, and Justifications* (Notre Dame, Indiana: University of Notre Dame Press, 1972); see also C. L. Ten, *Crime, Guilt and Punishment* (Oxford: Clarendon Press, 1987).
11. John Finnis relies on such ideas in his account of punishment as retributive. See his 'The Restoration of Retribution', *Analysis*, Vol. 32 (1972), and also Chapter 10 of his *Natural Law and Natural Rights* (Oxford: Clarendon Press, 1980).
12. Wesley Cragg, *The Practice of Punishment: Towards a Theory of Restorative Justice* (London: Routledge, 1992), understands restorative justice in this sense.
13. Richard Swinburne interprets John Locke to argue that the state when punishing acts as a representative of the victim of crime in exacting revenge. See his *Responsibility and Atonement* (Oxford: Clarendon Press, 1989), p. 94. See also my discussion of this issue in 'Punishment in Ireland: Can We Talk About It?', *Administration*, Vol. 41 (1993–94), pp. 347–61.

CHAPTER 2: AN ALTERNATIVE RATIONALITY

1. John Paul II, *Sollicitudo Rei Socialis* 1987 (London: Catholic Truth Society, 1988), para. 38. See also *The Logic of Solidarity: Commentaries on Pope John Paul II's Encyclical On Social Concern*, edited by Gregory Baum and Robert Ellsberg (New York: Orbis, 1989).
2. Joseph Heller, *Catch-22* (London: Corgi, 1964).
3. This scenario is presented in many versions, but here I borrow that presented in: J. R. Lucas, *On Justice* (Oxford: Clarendon Press, 1980), p. 46.
4. Garrett Hardin, *Collective Action* (Baltimore, Md.: Johns Hopkins University Press, 1982).
5. M. Hollis and E. Nell, *Rational Economic Man* (Cambridge: Cambridge University Press, 1975).
6. M. Hollis, *The Cunning of Reason* (Cambridge: Cambridge University Press, 1987).
7. Herman E. Daly and John B. Cobb Jr., *For the Common Good: Redirecting the Economy towards Community, the Environment and a Sustainable Future* (London: Green Print, 1990), document

instances of such anomalies.

8. J. L. Mackie, *Hume's Moral Theory* (London: Routledge and Kegan Paul, 1980).
9. Hollis, *Cunning of Reason*, p. 94.
10. I have discussed this at greater length in an article, 'The Philosophy of Action Science', *Journal of Managerial Psychology*, Vol. 10, No. 3 (1995), pp. 6–13.

CHAPTER 3: IS ALTRUISM THE KEY TO THE COMMON GOOD?

1. Ellen Frankel Paul, Fred D. Miller Jr. and Jeffrey Paul (eds.), *Altruism* (Cambridge: Cambridge University Press, 1993); see also Thomas Nagel, *The Possibility of Altruism* (Princeton: Princeton University Press, 1970).
2. Alasdair MacIntyre has a useful analysis of how the explanation and justification of altruism became the key issue for ethics in the eighteenth century. See his *After Virtue*, 2nd edn (Notre Dame, Indiana: University of Notre Dame Press, 1984), p. 229; also his *Whose Justice? Which Rationality?* (London: Duckworth, 1988), pp. 290f.
3. Or in another version of the same thought, their selfish genes are ensuring their reproductive success. Richard Dawkins has popularised this idea in his book, *The Selfish Gene*. See the survey article by Neven Sesardic, 'Recent Work on Human Altruism and Evolution', *Ethics*, Vol. 106 (1995), pp. 128–57.
4. David Schmidtz, 'Reasons for Altruism', in Frankel Paul et al. (eds.), *Altruism*, pp. 52–68.
5. Neera Kapur Badhwar, 'Altruism Versus Self-Interest: Sometimes a False Dichotomy', in Frankel Paul et al. (eds.), *Altruism*, pp. 90–117.
6. Christine M. Korsgaard, 'The Reasons We Can Share: An Attack on the Distinction between Agent-Relative and Agent-Neutral Values', in Frankel Paul et al. (eds.), *Altruism*, pp. 24–51.
7. Examples are Amitai Etzioni, *The Moral Dimension: Toward A New Economics* (New York: The Free Press, 1988); Jon Elster, *The Cement of Society: A Study of Social Order* (Cambridge: Cambridge University Press, 1989).
8. R. N. Bellah et al. (eds.), *Habits of the Heart: Individualism and Commitment in American Life* (Los Angeles: University of California Press, 1985).
9. This is the basic practical strategy behind Hobbes's covenant, Mill's liberty principle and Rawls's original position.
10. See William Kingston, 'Property Rights and the Making of Christendom', *Studies*, Vol. 82 (1993), pp. 402–25, at p. 425.
11. Jean Jacques Rousseau, *Discourse on the Origins of Inequality*,

edited by Michael L. Morgan (Indianapolis, Indiana: Hackett, 1992), p. 900.

CHAPTER 4: THE COMMON GOOD OF PRACTICES

1. I rely especially on his book, *After Virtue*, 2nd edn (Notre Dame, Indiana: University of Notre Dame Press, 1984).
2. See his 'Reply to Critics', in John Horton and Susan Mendus (eds.), *After MacIntyre* (Oxford: Polity Press, 1994).
3. Ibid., p. 285.
4. MacIntyre, *After Virtue*, p. 187.
5. Ibid., p. 194. See also his remarks in 'Reply', p. 288.
6. MacIntyre, *After Virtue*, p. 196.
7. MacIntyre, 'Reply', p. 284.
8. Ibid., p. 288.
9. Stephen Mulhall and Adam Swift, *Liberals and Communitarians* (Oxford: Blackwell, 1992).
10. This clarification was given in response to my question to him during the 1994 Agnes Cuming lectures at University College Dublin. He gave his series of three lectures the overall title: 'Laws, Goods, and Virtues: Medieval Resources for Modern Conflicts'. The second lecture bore the title: 'The Common Good Against the Nation State'.
11. MacIntyre, 'Reply', p. 303.
12. MacIntyre, *After Virtue*, p. 156.
13. Ibid., p. 232.
14. Ibid., p. 236.
15. Ibid., p. 253.
16. Ibid., p. 254.
17. Ibid., p. 255.
18. Ibid., p. 194.
19. Aristotle, *Politics*, Bk VII. See John M. Cooper, *Reason and Human Good in Aristotle* (Cambridge, Mass: Harvard University Press, 1975).
20. MacIntyre, *After Virtue*, p. 255.
21. Alasdair MacIntyre, *Whose Justice? Which Rationality?* (London: Duckworth, 1988), p. 119.
22. Aristotle, *Politics*, Bk I c. 2; Bk III cc 6, 9; Bk VII c. 13.
23. St Augustine, *The City of God*, edited by David Knowles (Harmondsworth: Penguin, 1972). See also: R. A. Markus, *Saeculum. History and Society in the Theology of St Augustine* (Cambridge: Cambridge University Press, 1970).
24. St Augustine, *City of God*, Bk XIX c. 6.
25. This is the point, I think, of John Rawls's recent book *Political Liberalism* (New York: Columbia University Press, 1993). Rawls

is attempting to answer criticisms of his earlier work, *A Theory of Justice*, to the effect that it failed as a general theory of moral justification. Rawls defends his theory by emphasising that it is designed to facilitate agreement by people on institutions and processes which enable them to coordinate their social life even though they are divided, and can be expected to remain divided, by disagreement in their world-views, moralities and interests. It is precisely a political rather than a general moral theory.

26. MacIntyre, *After Virtue*, p. 113.
27. Note awareness of this need as reflected in the papers collected in: R. Bruce Douglass et al. (eds.), *Liberalism and the Good* (New York: Routledge, 1990).
28. Aristotle, *Politics*, Bk III c. 9.

CHAPTER 5: ANOTHER LOOK AT PUBLIC ORDER

1. It is the prevalence of this point of view which lends plausibility to the sharp contrast drawn by Alasdair MacIntyre between the common good and the public interest, as discussed in the previous chapter.
2. J. L. Mackie, *Ethics: Inventing Right and Wrong* (Harmondsworth: Pelican, 1977); *Hume's Moral Theory* (London: Routledge and Kegan Paul, 1980).
3. Isaiah Berlin, 'Two Concepts of Liberty', in *Four Essays on Liberty* (Oxford: Oxford University Press, 1969).
4. Michael Novak, *Free Persons and the Common Good* (New York: Madison, 1989), pp. 113–18.
5. J. S. Mill, *On Liberty*, originally published 1858. I am using an edition by H. B. Acton (London: Dent, 1972); the quotation is from p. 78, emphasis mine.
6. Joel Feinberg, *Harm to Others*, Volume One of *The Moral Limits of the Criminal Law* (Oxford: Oxford University Press, 1984) explores the complexities of this allegedly simple principle.
7. I have taken this distinction from Trevor Pateman, *Language, Truth and Politics: Towards a Radical Theory for Communication*, 2nd edn (Lewes: Jean Stroud, 1980), pp. 161f.
8. Michele Dillon, *Debating Divorce: Moral Conflict in Ireland* (Lexington, KY: University Press of Kentucky, 1993), reviewed by me in *Studies*, Vol. 83 (Summer 1994), pp. 226–9.
9. R. M. Unger, *Knowledge and Politics* (New York: Free Press, 1975) offers a searching critique of such a liberal philosophy of law.
10. F. A. Hayek, *The Constitution of Liberty* (London: Routledge, 1960, reprinted 1976); also *Law, Legislation and Liberty: A New Statement of the Liberal Principles of Justice and Political Economy*,

paperback edition in one volume (London: Routledge, 1982).

11. Hayek, *Constitution*, p. 12.
12. Hayek, *Law* III, p. 8.
13. Hayek, *Constitution*, p. 487, n. 10.
14. Ibid., p. 154.
15. Hayek, *Law* III, p. 139.
16. Ibid., pp. 101f.
17. Ibid., p. 128.
18. Ibid., pp. 36f.
19. Ibid., pp. 66f.
20. See David Marquand, *The Unprincipled Society* (London: Fontana, 1989), who locates Britain's current difficulties in the lack of an adequate philosophy of the common good: self-interest cannot motivate the necessary cooperation.
21. Ibid., p. 80.
22. Mary Warnock, *A Question of Life: The Warnock Report on Human Fertilisation and Embryology* (Oxford: Blackwell, 1985), p. viii.
23. Ibid., p. xvi.
24. Ibid., p. 1.
25. Ibid., p. 3.
26. Ibid., pp. 96f.
27. Ibid., p. 99.
28. Ibid., p. xvi.
29. Ibid., p. x.
30. Ibid., pp. x, xvi.
31. Ibid., p. xii.
32. Ibid., p. div.
33. Ibid., pp. 2f.
34. Ibid., p. xiv, emphasis in original.
35. Ibid., p. xv.
36. This is presuming of course that the state is obliged to defend the rights of all and not simply those who are in a position to assert their rights.
37. Hannah Arendt, *The Human Condition* (Chicago: University of Chicago Press, 1958).
38. For an interesting discussion of how Hobbes's seemingly analytic science is also a rhetoric of persuasion, see Tom Sorell, 'Hobbes's Persuasive Civil Science', *The Philosophical Quarterly*, Vol. 40 (1990), pp. 342–51.

CHAPTER 6: RIGHTS AND PUBLIC ORDER

1. See Richard Tuck, *Natural Rights Theories, Their Origin and Development* (Cambridge: Cambridge University Press, 1979).
2. See John Finnis, *Natural Law and Natural Rights* (Oxford: Clarendon Press, 1980), pp. 286f.

3. *Instruction on Christian Freedom and Liberation* (Washington, DC: United States Catholic Conference, 1986), para. 85.
4. Ibid.
5. John Paul II, *Sollicitudo Rei Socialis* (London: Catholic Truth Society, 1988). See the discussion above in Chapter 2.
6. These distinctions, which were first developed by the American jurist W. N. Hohfeld, are discussed by Finnis in Chapter 8 of *Natural Law and Natural Rights*.
7. Paul Sieghart documents the disagreements in interpretation of Article 23(1) of the Universal Declaration of Human Rights which asserts 'Everyone has the right to work'. See his *The Lawful Rights of Mankind: An Introduction to the International Legal Code of Human Rights* (Oxford: Oxford University Press, 1985), Chapter 13: 'Work, Income and Property'.
8. See The Linacre Centre, *Euthanasia and Clinical Practice: Trends, Principles and Alternatives. The Report of a Working Party* (London: The Linacre Centre, 1982).
9. VES documentation, as for instance, The Voluntary Euthanasia Society, *Newsletter*, No. 3 (Dec. 1984), London.

CHAPTER 7: THE DEBATE ON THE HUMAN GOOD

1. Michael Novak, *Free Persons and the Common Good* (New York: Madison, 1989).
2. Alasdair MacIntyre, *Whose Justice? Which Rationality?* (London: Duckworth, 1988), pp. 344f.
3. Two recent publications by groups of political philosophers within the liberal tradition reflect this growing awareness and concern. *Liberalism and the Good* edited by R. Bruce Douglass, Gerald M. Mara and Henry S. Richardson (New York: Routledge, 1990); *The Good Life and the Human Good* edited by Ellen Frankel Paul, Fred D. Miller Jr. and Jeffrey Paul (Cambridge: Cambridge University Press, 1992).
4. John Rawls, *Political Liberalism* (New York: Columbia University Press, 1993), p. 181; see *A Theory of Justice* (Oxford: Oxford University Press, 1972), pp. 13–14, 144–5.
5. The priority given to liberty is the reason why the classification of Rawls as an egalitarian liberal is not quite accurate. However, from the perspective of Nozick who is much more libertarian in his approach, Rawls is prepared to limit freedom for the sake of equality, outlawing 'capitalist acts between consenting adults'!
6. Rawls, *Political Liberalism*, p. 202.
7. Martha Nussbaum, 'Aristotelian Social Democracy', in Douglass et al. (eds.), *Liberalism and the Good*, pp. 203–52.

8. Her use of 'thick' and 'thin' is consistent with Rawls's earlier usage, but not his later. 'Thick' is correlated with ends, and 'thin' is correlated with means. The identification of ends capable of receiving agreement among participants is achieved by use of the qualifier 'vague'.
9. Ibid., p. 219.
10. This passage is my summary of her longer list, ibid., p. 225.
11. There are interesting parallels between Nussbaum's list and the list of basic forms of human good proposed by John Finnis in *Natural Law and Natural Rights* (Oxford: Clarendon Press, 1980), Chapters 3 and 4. Not surprising perhaps, since both authors are attempting a reworking of Aristotle.
12. Attracta Ingram's proposal of a political theory of rights, to which I referred in the Introduction, is another example of this procedure. She discusses the notion of autonomy as providing a normative descriptive of the human which serves as a moral basis for her political theory. See her *A Political Theory of Rights* (Oxford: Oxford University Press, 1994), Chapter 5. My suggestion is that a shared understanding and valuing of autonomy is a common good of a liberal political culture, as much as the institutions maintaining and protecting rights.

CHAPTER 8: SECURING A PUBLIC SPACE

1. *Love is for Life*, Irish Bishops' Pastoral (Dublin: Veritas, 1985), paragraph 187. An appendix reproduces statements made in the context of earlier debates.
2. See Austin Flannery (ed.), *Vatican Council II: The Conciliar and Post Conciliar Documents* (New York: Costello, 1975), p. 800.
3. Patrick Hannon, *Church, State, Morality and Law* (Dublin: Gill and Macmillan, 1992), Chapter 7.
4. Aquinas, *Summa Theologiae*, translated by Blackfriars (London: Eyre and Spottiswoode, 1966), Vol. XXVIII, Ia IIae, q.96 a.2.
5. Ibid., q.96 a.3.
6. Ibid., q.92 a.1.
7. Ibid., q.92 a.1 ad3m.
8. Ibid., q.95 a.1.
9. See Hannon, *Church, State, Morality and Law* for a discussion of these issues.

CHAPTER 9: DISCOURSE AND THE PROCESS OF POLITICS

1. Alasdair MacIntyre, *Whose Justice? Which Rationality?* (London: Duckworth, 1988), p. 336.
2. William Kingston discusses the franchise as a counterbalance

to other property rights in his article: 'Property Rights and the Making of Christendom', *Studies*, Vol. 82 (1993), pp. 402–25.

3. Alasdair MacIntyre, *After Virtue*, 2nd edn (Notre Dame, Indiana: University of Notre Dame Press, 1984), p. 253.
4. Jürgen Habermas, *Reason and the Rationalisation of Society*, translated and introduced by T. McCarthy (London: Heinemann, 1979).
5. Habermas is not the only philosopher exploring the possibilities of constructing a social philosophy based on the analysis of discourse. A similar attempt is made by another German, Oswald Schwemmer, whose work I have presented elsewhere. See my *The Practical Philosophy of Oswald Schwemmer* (Lanham, Maryland: University Press of America, 1991).
6. See Michael Pusey, *Jürgen Habermas*, Key Sociologists Series (London: Tavistock, 1987).
7. Stephen K. White, *The Recent Work of Jürgen Habermas: Reason, Justice and Modernity* (Cambridge: Cambridge University Press, 1988), p. 53.
8. Jürgen Habermas, *Moralbewußtsein und kommunikatives Handeln* (Frankfurt am Main: Suhrkamp, 1983).
9. Ibid., p. 99, quoted by White, *Recent Work*, p. 56.
10. Following Frederick A. Olafson, 'Habermas as a Philosopher', *Ethics*, Vol. 100 (1990), pp. 641–57, at p. 651.
11. Simone Chambers, 'Discourse and Democratic Practices', *The Cambridge Companion to Habermas*, edited by Stephen K. White (Cambridge: Cambridge University Press, 1995), pp. 233–59. She is relying on Habermas's treatment of the issue in *Faktizität und Geltung: Beiträge zur Diskurstheorie des Rechts und des demokratischen Rechtsstaats* (Frankfurt am Main: Suhrkamp, 1992).
12. Chambers, 'Discourse and Democratic Practices', p. 242.
13. Ibid., p. 238.
14. Ibid., p. 246.
15. Ibid., p. 247.
16. Ibid., p. 239.
17. MacIntyre, *After Virtue*, p. 187.

CHAPTER 10: THE LANGUAGE OF THE COMMON GOOD

1. For instance, Martha Nussbaum, 'Aristotelian Social Democracy', in *Liberalism and the Good* edited by R. Bruce Douglass et al. (New York: Routledge, 1990); also Douglas Rasmussen and Douglas Den Uyl, *Liberty and Nature: An Aristotelian Defense of Liberal Order* (La Salle, Illinois: Open Court, 1991).

2. See for instance Anthony Kenny, *Aristotle on the Perfect Life* (Oxford: Clarendon Press, 1992), especially Chapter 4: 'Friendship and Self-love'; also Paul J. Wadell, *Friendship and the Moral Life* (Notre Dame, Indiana: University of Notre Dame Press, 1989).

3. John Finnis, *Natural Law and Natural Rights* (Oxford: Clarendon Press, 1980), Chapter 6.

4. This is the kind of cooperation which is prone to the free-rider problem discussed in Chapter 2.

5. Finnis, *Natural Law*, pp. 139f.

6. Ibid., p. 140.

7. Alasdair MacIntyre, *After Virtue*, 2nd edn (Notre Dame, Indiana: University of Notre Dame Press, 1984), p. 258.

8. Ibid., p. 288.

9. Aristotle, *Politics*, Bk 1 c. 2.

10. See Thomas Hobbes, *Leviathan*, c. 17; also David K. Lewis, *Convention: A Philosophical Study* (Cambridge, Mass: Harvard University Press, 1969), pp. 88–97; note that Aristotle in his *Politics* was aware of the possibility of viewing political community as a business deal, either for the sake of profit or for the sake of (military) security (Bk III c. 9).

11. Plato, *The Republic*, Bk I 343b–c, 345c.

12. The recognition given to certain individuals for their contribution to public life reflects this understanding that they are to be thanked for the benefits they have brought to society. Thanks is given on the assumption that the benefits were intended out of concern. Think of the acknowledgement of the contributions of Noel Browne to the treatment of TB, of T. K. Whitaker to the introduction of economic planning, of John Hume to the advancement of the peace process, of Brian Walsh to the evolution of the jurisprudence of rights in the Supreme Court.

13. Jean Jacques Rousseau, *The Social Contract*, Bk III c. 15.

14. Para. 74, quoted in Rodger Charles SJ, *The Social Teaching of Vatican II* (San Francisco: Ignatius, 1982), p. 207.

INDEX

A

abortion, 59, 98-100, 106, 107, 129
After Virtue (MacIntyre), 59-61
altruism, 4
  combined with self-interest, 48-9
  and the common good, 44-9
  and egoism, 54
  in moral philosophy, 45-7
Aquinas, St Thomas, 131-5
Arendt, Hannah, 100
Aristotle, 48, 61, 64, 91, 116, 122, 123, 133
  adapting, 71-4
  Finnis version of, 155-63
  virtue and the state, 65, 66-7
Augustine, St, 67-8, 69, 71, 116, 133

B

bargaining, 137, 139-40, 152
Bellah, Robert N., 57
Binchy, William, 89
business relations, 158-9, 161-2

C

Catch-22, 29-30
Catholic Church, 2, 135
  on common good, 129
  learning from Mill and Aquinas, 131-5
  and moral debates, 130-1
  social teaching, 109-10
Chambers, Simone, 146-8, 149, 151
Church, State, Morality and Law

(Hannon), 130
City of God (Augustine), 67-8
civil liberties, 79-80
civil war, 60, 81-3, 138-9
claim-rights, 110-11
coercion, 39
common good. *see also* language
  altruism key to, 44-9
  analogical conception of, 164
  human good, 108-9, 116-26
  institutions as, 70-1
  language of, 153-70
  locating problem of, 6-27
  meaning of, 154-5
  neutrality on, 90-100
  and penal system, 10-13
  of practices, 50-75
  process of politics as, 149-51
  and public order, 4-5, 72-4, 128
  and punishment, 18-19
  rationale for, 29-30
  'sectarian' concept, 2-3
  and state, 25, 57-61, 77
Common Good, The (Jordan), 9
communicative action, 152
  versus strategic action, 144-5
  theory of, 141-4
communitarians, 57-8, 65-6
community, 68
  complete community, 157, 161-3
  cooperation in, 50-5, 76
  practices in, 150
compassion, loss of, 7-9
Constitution of Ireland, 1-2, 100
contraception, 129

cooperation, 3, 4, 27, 146-7
  analysis of, 7-10
  business relations, 158-9, 161-2
  complete community, 161-3
  explanations of, 76-8, 101-3
  friendship, 159-60
  goods of, 66
  play relations, 159, 162
  practices, 50-75
  rationality of, 36-41, 155-8, 166-7
  and self-interest, 165-6
corruption, 54-5, 56, 76
crime
  civil war model, 24
  game-restoration model, 22-3
Criminal Justice and the Pursuit of Decency (Rutherford), 10-13
Cunning of Reason, The (Hollis), 36

D
Debating Divorce: Moral Conflict in Ireland (Dillon), 89-90
Declaration on Religious Liberty, 130-1, 134-5
democracy, 83, 94, 132
  pluralism, 98-100
Dillon, Michele, 89
discourse
  Habermas on, 141-4
  and process of politics, 136-52
divorce, 89-90, 106, 107, 129

E
embryo research, 95-8
Enlightenment, 69, 131, 140-1, 152
  concern for rationality, 137, 169-70
  language of rights, 105
  optimism of, 150
environment, 34-6, 38

Ethics: Inventing Right and Wrong (Mackie), 80
Etzioni, Amitai, 57
euthanasia, 113, 115
Evangelium Vitae, 2
exclusion, 24
external goods, 51-4, 56

F
Finnis, John, 155-63
  application of analysis, 163-7
fisheries control, 34-5, 38
fishing, 160
free-rider paradox, 37-8, 59
French Revolution, 105
Freud, Sigmund, 6
friendship, 156, 157, 159-60, 161
  model of, 162

G
games theory, 32-4
Gaudium et Spes, 166
government, 137, 162
  limits on, 84-5
  MacIntyre on, 60

H
Habermas, Jürgen, 140-1, 148, 149, 151-2
  theory of communicative action, 141-4
Hannon, Patrick, 130-1
Hardin, Garrett, 35
Hayek, Frederick, 91, 92-4, 97, 102
Heller, Joseph, 29-30
history, 69-70, 73-4
Hobbes, Thomas, 141
  on cooperation, 38-9, 40-1
  language of rights, 105
  on public order, 79-80, 81-3, 102, 136
  on punishment, 21
  rationale of the state, 60, 66, 67

Hollis, Martin, 36-42
homosexuality, 129
human good, 108-9, 152, 154, 156, 168-9
  debate on, 116-26
  neutrality, 116-17
  thick, vague theory of, 122-5, 128
  thin theory of, 118-22
human rights. *see* rights
Hume, David, 39-40, 60, 66, 81, 127
Hume's Moral Theory (Mackie), 80

I
individualism, 20-1, 111
Ingram, Attracta, 3
institutions, 74-5, 121, 135, 146, 154
  as goods, 61-4, 70-1, 168-9
  MacIntyre on, 55-6
  and organisations, 63-4
Instruction on Christian Freedom and Liberation, 109
interest groups, 137-40, 165-6
internal goods, 51-4, 56-7

J
John Paul II, Pope, 28-9
Jordan, Bill, 9

K
Kant, Immanuel, 40, 105

L
law, 76, 78-84
  and Catholic Church, 131-5
  and the good, 91-2
  moral debates, 106, 129-31
  need for public space, 127-35
  relation of moral to legal rights, 111-13
  thin theory of the good, 118-22

Leviathan (Hobbes), 38-9, 40-1, 79, 81-3
liberalism
  and Aristotelianism, 71-4
  and Catholic Church, 131-5
  neutral on human good, 117-18
  practice of discourse, 150-1
  protection of liberty, 84-90
  and rationality, 136-7, 169-70
  thick, vague theory, 122-5
  thin theory, 118-22
  without relativism, 87-8
liberation, 84-5
liberties, 92-4
  abortion as question of recognition, 98-100
  and claim-rights, 110-11
  distinctions of, 84-5
  embryo research, 95-8
  'harm to others' principle, 88-90
  Mill on, 85-8
  pluralism, 125
  problems of order and freedom, 94-5
  protection by state, 76-8, 79, 84-90, 101-3, 116
  and public order, 113-14
Locke, John, 21, 136, 141
  limitations on government, 84-5, 105
  rationale of the state, 60, 66

M
McCarroll, Joe, 89-90
MacIntyre, Alasdair, 116
  on bargaining, 137, 139-40, 152
  on cooperation, 159, 160
  criticism of, 61-75
  on institutions, 55-6
  on liberalism, 117-18
  on moral debate, 59-61
  politics and conflict, 66-74

on practices, 50-61, 150
on virtue, 53-6, 72, 73
Mackie, John L., 39, 80-1
Marx, Karl, 6
medical profession, 52-3
military force, 59
Mill, John Stuart, 131-5, 136
    'harm to others' principle, 88-90
    protection of liberty, 77, 85-8, 102, 104, 127, 128
    rationale of the state, 60, 66
minimalism, 164-5, 169
moral debates, 5, 106, 107-8, 129-31, 154, 169
    need for public space, 127-35
    personal autonomy, 108-9
moral vacuum, 59-61
myth, 123, 126

N
nationalism, 49
Nell, E., 36
New Ireland Forum, 130
Novak, Michael, 84-5
Nozick, Robert, 118
Nussbaum, Martha, 122-6

O
objectification, 81
On Liberty (Mill), 85-8
organisations, 63-4

P
Paine, Thomas, 105
Paul, Ellen Frankel, 44
penal system, 10-13, 26
planning laws, 138-9
Plato, 67
play relations, 159, 161-2
Political Liberalism (Rawls), 1, 120-1
politics
    and Catholic Church, 131-5
    common good in, 71-4
    and conflict, 66-74

cooperation, 162-3
process of, 136-52
    bargaining, not argument, 137
    as a common good, 149-51
    communicative action, 141-5
    idiom of, 137-41
    rational politics?, 146-8
    theory of communicative action, 141-4
Politics (Aristotle), 72-4
practices, 4, 56-7, 76, 135, 154
    common good of, 50-75
    in community, 150
    and institutions, 62
    internal/external goods, 51-4
'prisoners' dilemma', 31-4
projection, 81
property distribution, 59
prostitution, 112, 115
public order, 69-71, 76-103, 140, 154, 168. *see also* law
    and the common good, 4-5, 72-4, 128
    and rights, 104-15
public service, 162-3
public space, 154, 169
    securing, 127-35
punishment, 4, 13-25, 167-8
    models of
        applied to social experience, 22-4
        and common good, 18-19
        correction, 15-16, 18
        other models, 19-22
        restoration, 16-18
    penal system, 10-13

R
rationality, 127, 136-7, 168
    alternative, 28-43, 140
    and altruism, 45-7
    and compassion, 8-9
    discourse, 141-4, 146-8

examined, 36-41
models of, 9-10, 153
practice and theory, 41-3
of self-interest, 31-6
two kinds of, 144-5
Rawls, John, 1, 126, 137
theory of the good, 118-22
reciprocity, 142
relativism, 87-8
revolutions, 105
rights, 3-4, 5, 83-4
autonomy of self, 107, 108-9, 115
claim-rights, 110-11
language of, 104-6, 127
and public order, 104-15
relation of moral to legal rights, 111-13
resort to language of, 107-8
right to work, 109-10
Rousseau, Jean Jacques, 50, 165
on punishment, 21
on self-interest, 7-9, 10, 28, 48-9
Rutherford, Andrew, 10-13, 26

S
Sandel, Michael J., 57
science, language of, 6-8, 28, 42-3
Second Vatican Council, 132
sectarianism, 2-3, 128, 170
self-interest, 4, 47, 95
analysis of actions, 47-8
and cooperation, 44
how to combine with other-interest, 48-9
limitations of, 168
rationality of, 31-6
current issues, 34-6
'prisoners' dilemma', 31-4
Rousseau on, 7-9, 10
self-protection, 86
Smith, Adam, 85
social goods, 4-5, 22-4, 118-22
social systems, 145

Sollicitudo Rei Socialis, 28-9
sovereign, role of, 82-3, 105
sport, 159
correction within, 16-18
state. *see also* politics; public order
common good against, 57-61
as community, 161
function of discourse in, 146-7
law and order, 25, 76-7, 78-84
and liberties, 101-3
neutral on the good, 77, 90-100
protection of liberty, 76-8, 84-90
role of, 25, 59-61, 116
self-interest in, 165-6
and virtue, 65-9
Stephens, James Fitzjames, 11
strategic action, 144-5, 152
suicide, 112-13, 114, 115

T
teaching profession, 52-3, 62
Theory of Justice, A (Rawls), 119-20, 121
tolerance, 88
trades unions, 137
'tragedy of the commons', 35-6, 42
trust, 40-1

V
Vatican II, 130-1, 134-5
victim
state as agent for, 25
support for, 13, 20-1
vigilantes, 20
virtue, 64-5
and modern state, 53-6, 72-4
Voluntary Euthanasia Society, 113, 114

W
Warnock, Mary, 95-8
work, right to, 109-10